T0104085

GARDENING for KIDS

GARDENING for KIDS

Learn, Grow, and Get Messy with Fun STEAM Projects

BY BRANDY STONE

Illustrated by Katy Dockrill

callisto
publishing
an imprint of Sourcebooks

Copyright © 2020 by Callisto Publishing LLC

Cover and internal design © 2020 by Callisto Publishing LLC

Illustrations © 2020 Katy Dockrill. Pattern vector created by freepik - www.freepik.com.

Author photo courtesy of Kayenta Stone.

Interior and Cover Designer: Richard Tapp

Art Producer: Sara Feinstein

Editor: Ada Fung

Production Editor: Emily Sheehan

Callisto Kids and the colophon are registered trademarks of Callisto Publishing LLC.

All rights reserved. No part of this book may be reproduced in any form or by any electronic or mechanical means including information storage and retrieval systems—except in the case of brief quotations embodied in critical articles or reviews—without permission in writing from its publisher, Sourcebooks LLC.

All brand names and product names used in this book are trademarks, registered trademarks, or trade names of their respective holders. Callisto Publishing is not associated with any product or vendor in this book.

Published by Callisto Publishing LLC C/O Sourcebooks LLC

P.O. Box 4410, Naperville, Illinois 60567-4410

(630) 961-3900

callistopublishing.com

This product conforms to all applicable CPSC and CPSIA standards.

Source of Production: 1010 Printing Asia Limited, Kwun Tong, Hong Kong, China

Date of Production: January 2024

Run Number: 5035734

Printed and bound in China

OGP 2

TO THE GARDENERS FROM MY CHILDHOOD—
Dad, Mom, Memie, Aunt JoAnn, Kirsty, AND Alice.

Contents

A Note for Parents and Educators

- -

This book is filled with questions, observations, and fascinating facts about gardening and nature. The projects and experiments in this book are a result of my own curiosity and admiration for plants and creatures. The natural world deeply influences my work as a photographer, educator, and writer. I have seen the physical, mental, and educational benefits of gardening with kids, both for my own children and for the children I have taught in my nature-based children's programs.

Gardening provides the perfect setting for STEAM-based learning (science, technology, engineering, art, and math). STEAM-based learning involves teaching two or more of these subjects combined in one project. For me, the STEAM approach to education feels like being taught by nature: It is complex, integrated, and always interesting! The STEAM projects in this book guide children ages 8 to 12 through fun, garden-based learning. You are the best judge of your child's abilities and can decide which projects are best suited for them. Most projects are easy to modify for kids who may be a little younger or older than the suggested age range. Before starting a project, read through it to see if there are any caution notes or prep work that should be done ahead of time.

The first chapter in this book is for educators, parents, and guardians. It has tips on how to safely and successfully garden with kids, whether you are gardening in a group setting or at home. It also has specific ideas for educators. There are additional helpful resources at the back of the book, including a blank gardening journal and a team activity sheet that can be copied and used for group projects.

I am excited for you to explore the pages of this book and, ultimately, share the joy of gardening with a child. This book is close to my heart because gardening fills me with wonder, helps me feel part of an interconnected world, and ignites hundreds of questions I want answers for—just like a child.

A Note for Budding Gardeners

When I was a child, I dreamed about rolling down grassy, green hills and pushing through large jungle leaves. Plants, especially lush, green plants covering the landscape, were an unfamiliar and unexplored territory. I lived in a dry desert. The natural landscape was mostly rocks, sand, and spiky plants. But there was plenty of sunlight and warmth, and I discovered that as soon as you add water, the desert comes alive with plant life and color. Gardening in the desert was like performing a magic trick—dry land could be transformed into a green world. I was captivated!

Digging and planting give me a chance to create art with nature, and I love it! Gardening is also a way to explore science while playing with dirt. Spending just a few moments in a garden can lead to new discoveries. This book is filled with 25 gardening-themed projects and experiments you can do with a parent, teacher, or other adults. You will explore fascinating concepts in science, technology, engineering, art, and math (called STEAM) when you dig into these gardening activities. For example, if you make your own mini-greenhouse, you'll combine art, engineering, science, and technology to make the perfect environment for a seed to grow. I hope you enjoy creating art with nature and seeking out science with this book!

How to Use This Book

- -

In chapter 1 (for adults) you'll find:

Inspiration for sharing gardening with kids: Discover the benefits of gardening and the STEAM approach to learning, plus ideas about why and how to garden with kids.

Safety tips: Learn ways to reduce risks and safely supervise kids in a garden.

Top tips for gardening with kids: Foster a fun, positive gardening experience with these teaching techniques and gardening tips.

How to choose the best project: Use this reference guide to choose the best project for yourself, with a chart of considerations like group size, age range, and time of year.

Garden classroom tips: Try these ideas for engaging larger groups of students in a classroom setting.

In chapter 2 (for kids) you'll find:

STEAM in the garden: Find out how you can explore science, technology, engineering, art, and math through gardening and playing in the dirt!

Interesting facts about plants: Explore a plant's life cycle and the parts of a plant.

Helpful gardening skills: Learn everything from how to plant a seed to how to water your garden so you can garden with confidence.

The best tools and easy-to-grow plants: Discover what gardening tools you'll need, plus the best plants to grow.

Ground rules for safety in the garden: Study up on how to keep safe while gardening.

In the back of the book you'll find:

Blank gardening record templates: Use these to make a gardening journal, record results of experiments, or assign gardening tasks. You can either photocopy the pages or download printable copies at CallistoMedia.com/gardeningforkids.

Resources: Find additional sources to learn more about gardening and places to purchase gardening tools and materials.

Project Features

STEAM Circles: Those displayed in full color show which STEAM subject the project covers (science, technology, engineering, art, or math).

Time of Year: Indicates what season is best for the project.

Difficulty Level: Indicates how much adult supervision might be needed. **Easy** projects can be done with little or no adult involvement. **Medium** projects may require some adult help. **Advanced** projects are the most challenging, and adult assistance is needed.

Dirt-O-Meter: Notes whether the mess level (digging, soil, and water involvement) is **high** or **low**.

Project Time: The time required to complete the prep work for a project, the project itself, and to see results.

Grow Time: The approximate time needed for a project to grow to maturity.

Caution!: Important safety warnings that indicate when adult supervision or assistance might be required.

Tools List: Lists the tools needed for the project.

Materials List: Lists the supplies and ingredients needed for the project.

I DIG IT!

I Dig It!: This box explains how the project highlights a particular gardening concept.

STEAM CONNECTION

STEAM Connection: This box explains one of the STEAM concepts in the project in more detail.

Mix It Up: A tip on how to vary the project.

For a Group: A tip for scaling up or dividing a project so that it can be used in a group setting.

Keep in Mind: A tip on things to consider or look out for while doing the project.

Part I

GROW, PLAY, LEARN

Ready to dig in? Before getting out your trowel and seeds, give this part a read so that you're well prepared for your gardening adventures! Chapter 1 is directed at adults; it provides tips for how to garden safely with kids and how to select the right gardening project—whether you're a parent of one gardening in a backyard or a teacher building a classroom garden. Chapter 2 is for kids; it will teach them basic plant science terms and gardening skills, as well as lay out a few gardening rules to follow.

The Hows and Whys of Gardening with Kids

The garden is nature's laboratory—it sparks imagination and ingenuity and kindles a desire to question and learn in anyone brave enough to enter the world of soil, roots, and sunlight. Many of you may already have the gardening bug and know how rewarding and fulfilling it can be. But you might be wondering how to get your kids involved and how to garden with them safely and still have fun. This chapter will answer your questions and give you useful tips and inspiration for gardening with kids.

Why Garden with Kids?

The garden offers much more than delicious fruit, colorful flowers, and nutritious vegetables. While growing and gathering, children also harvest a multitude of health benefits and scientific and social skills. Activities like carrying large watering cans, pushing a wheelbarrow, and moving soil or rocks not only help strengthen muscles, but studies show they also help kids stay calm and focused. In a garden, kids have the freedom to explore and discover things on their own. This kind of freedom leads to independence and confidence. Spending time looking, listening, feeling, smelling, and tasting what is growing in the ground connects kids to nature and engages all of their senses.

Beyond play and exercise, gardening also presents kids with the opportunity to learn about and apply science, technology, engineering, art, and math (STEAM) concepts and skills. The STEAM approach to education integrates all of these disciplines rather than teaching them separately. In STEAM-based learning, kids apply creative thinking and the scientific method to real-world problem-solving. Best of all, studies have found that children are more likely to retain what they have learned after doing STEAM-based projects.

The projects and experiments in this book embrace the STEAM approach—they get kids involved in and proactive about their learning and development, all while having fun and getting messy in the garden! Gardening and experiencing the life cycle of plants gives children the satisfaction of caring for something over time. Planning and maintaining a garden with friends or family gives kids an opportunity to share their creativity, ideas, and opinions. Kids are naturals at observing, wondering, investigating, and experimenting, and nurturing those skills will serve them well throughout their lives. Making mistakes and solving problems help kids face challenges on their own. Gardening can teach them that unexpected observations—and even failures—result in new questions for further study. Children won't even know they are being scientists, engineers, or artists: They'll just be having fun!

BE OKAY WITH THE MESS AND THE MESS-UPS

Do you dread the mess that comes with letting kids loose in the garden? Are you worried about crooked rows, unwanted holes, and that kids might pull up more plants than they grow? It's okay—you're not alone! These are common concerns for many parents. But it's the digging in and getting dirty that will make the biggest impact on kids' understanding of how to make their garden grow. A single, notable discovery made while making a mess becomes a memorable learning moment. And in the long run, kids who are given room to make messes and mistakes will become more resilient and responsible. So, take a deep breath and try to accept the chaos—you might not always succeed, and that's okay, too! Here are some tips for managing the mess:

◆ Check the Dirt-O-Meter ratings before starting a project or experiment. If you aren't in the mood for muddy mayhem, choose something with a *low* rating.

◆ Whether you are using containers or growing in the ground, section off a spot where kids can have free rein to give them a safe zone to create messes.

◆ Make cleanup a part of gardening by having a "leave-it-as-you-found-it" rule. Returning things to where they belong and cleaning off surfaces together makes it easy to say "yes" to the next mess!

Safety First!

Gardening invites exploration and active play. While it is a relatively low-risk outdoor activity, it's still essential to take some safety precautions. This includes making sure the area you are working in is safe, supervising gardening activities, and defining safety rules. The following tips can help you create an inviting space for children by reducing harmful exposures and risky conditions.

Establishing a Safe Environment

◆ Lock chemicals and sharp tools away; do not allow children to use them unsupervised.

◆ Use gardening gloves to protect kids' hands while using tools or when they are helping with thorny plants.

◆ Make sure children can identify local poisonous or dangerous plants, insects, and wildlife. Talk with them about how to avoid stings and bites and what to do if they encounter an aggressive species.

◆ Carefully research all plants brought into the garden to avoid poisonous or irritant varieties. Remove plants that can cause allergic reactions, stings, or rashes.

◆ Consider relocating sharp or thorny plants from areas where kids will be active.

◆ Fence off steep banks, ponds, and any dangerous openings that kids could fall or crawl into.

◆ Provide protection from the heat and sun, including sunblock, UV-blocking hats, shaded areas, and plenty of water.

Supervising While Gardening

◆ Read through the projects ahead of time so you know what to expect and check the ⚠ warnings for each project for important safety concerns.

◆ Never leave young children alone outside.

◆ Show children how to use tools and equipment.

◆ When heavy lifting or the use of sharp tools is needed, prepare the site ahead of time.

◆ Safety should be the goal of supervision. Step in to help a child if there is a danger of injury. Redirect them to a safe place and explain what the danger was.

◆ Promote independence and free exploration by stepping in to help only when a child is in a situation they cannot handle alone. If possible, encourage them to try to work through the problem first, allowing them to grow from the experience.

Set Rules for Kids to Follow

◆ Look through the Dos and Don'ts section in chapter 2 (page 22) for help with establishing your own rules.
◆ Provide motivation for following rules. For example, remind them that they get more freedom to explore if they follow the rules. If they do not follow the rules, they must stay close by your side.
◆ Include rules that foster positive behavior like teamwork, cooperation, talking through conflicts, and sharing. Praise positive behavior whenever you notice it.
◆ Post the rules in an area where kids can see them. This gives them a voice in resolving problems they might encounter.

Top Tips for Gardening with Kids

After establishing safe practices for gardening, it's time to dig in and start having fun! Here are a few tips to help get you started on your gardening adventure.

Pick the Right Project

The first step toward creating a fun, positive experience is to plan for your unique circumstances. If you're starting a garden from scratch with your kids, consider what type of garden you want, where it will go, how large it will be, and whether to use containers or a garden bed. Some considerations when choosing a project include the time of year, the number of kids involved, their ages and attention spans, and how much time you have for a project. The Which Project Is Right for Us? chart on page 8 can help you choose a good one.

Keep It Simple

Starting a garden shouldn't be overwhelming. Plant the seeds of curiosity by starting small and slowly building basic gardening knowledge with children. Stick with one or two simple concepts or plants in the beginning, and let kids take time to experiment and master their growing skills; this helps foster the desire to keep trying. As they gain experience, they may naturally want to explore more advanced techniques.

Know Your Climate

Mother Nature can throw a lot of surprises at a gardener. You can minimize setbacks by understanding what types of plants grow well in your climate. Yes, if you live in the desert, your kid might be disappointed to know that they won't be able to grow a grove of banana trees, but they will have a better chance of good results if they start with local plants. Teach kids that every climate has its own set of conditions that help some crops flourish while other crops struggle. Help them look into your local average temperatures, seasonal weather patterns, rainfall, sunlight, and soil quality. See the Resources section on page 122 for where to find climate information.

Grow Your Favorites

Homegrown food tastes fantastic, so why not grow the flavors you love? Focusing on favorite foods and plants will increase the excitement and enjoyment kids experience in the garden. Consider saving seeds from your most-loved vegetables and sprouting them.

Encourage Individual Creativity and Exploration

Raising self-motivated, curious, and creative children starts with giving them the freedom to investigate things on their own, and the garden is a great place for that. Nature offers perfect specimens for exploring color, shape, line, texture, and space.

Encourage children to observe small details by using a magnifying glass, taking close-up images with a camera, or doing leaf rubbings. Give children the freedom to explore their own ideas by showing them a few techniques and then letting them create on their own. This could include creating artistic sculptures and images out of things found in nature: Look at Foraged Petal and Leaf Creatures (page 97) and Floral Photography Studio (page 100) for examples. Or read stories about the inspiring people who invented the wheelbarrow, greenhouse, flowerpot, and trellis. A garden is a perfect environment for young inventors and artists to bloom!

Foster Community and Connection

Gardening in groups at school or with friends and family at home is a great way to feel a sense of belonging. While planning, managing, and harvesting together, take the opportunity to teach children how to respect others' opinions and ideas, how to reach a consensus, and how to be a responsible member of a group. Gardening is an inclusive activity. Anyone can nurture plants and perform garden experiments, no matter their race, economic status, academic standing, background, age, abilities, or talents. Promote inclusivity by forming a diverse group. Children can also feel a strengthened sense of community by donating a portion of their harvest to local food banks, shelters, and even small animal rehabilitation centers.

Share Your Enthusiasm

Children get excited when they can share your enthusiasm. Point out your favorite flower color, admire a fuzzy bee, smell fragrant herbs, taste freshly picked strawberries, and talk about things you are personally passionate about. Curiosity is contagious, and the garden is filled with endless possibilities for exploring together. Show them what brings you joy in the garden. Give kids an enthusiastic companion and they will happily join you!

Which Project Is Right for Us?

CONSIDERATION	PROJECT/EXPERIMENT	OTHER IDEAS
INDOOR PROJECT	Sprout-Test Old Seeds (page 40) Food-Scrap Sprouting (page 63) Amazing Plant Race (page 77) Herb and Flower Drying Rack (page 109) The Grand Grape Jam Quest (page 106)	Make seed bombs. Create an herb centerpiece. Build a terrarium in a jar.
OUTDOOR CLASS GARDEN OR COMMUNITY GARDEN	Space-Saving Spiral Garden (page 55) Leaf Color Change (page 37) Worm Tower Soil Conditioner (page 88) Do Your Tomatoes Need a Best Friend? (page 81) Assemble a Team of Garden Superheroes (page 84) The "Water Less, Worry Less" Self-Watering System (page 74) Ribbon-Wrapped Plant Fort (page 70)	Start a classroom compost bin. Construct a pizza-shaped garden design and section off "slices" for growing different types of veggies for pizza toppings. Make a rain barrel to water the garden.
QUICK TIME FRAME	Root Study (page 67) The Incredible Leveling Tube (page 46) Mud Shower Water-Flow Test (page 31) Simple Fizzy Soil Test (page 28) Strawberry Salsa Science (page 103) Foraged Petal and Leaf Creatures (page 97)	Make plant labels or garden signs. Practice flower arranging. Print with chlorophyll on paper or T-shirts.

CONSIDERATION	PROJECT/EXPERIMENT	OTHER IDEAS
YOUNG CHILDREN	Root Study (page 67) Sprout-Test Old Seeds (page 40) Food-Scrap Sprouting (page 63) Foraged Petal and Leaf Creatures (page 97) Garden-Grown Pigment Paint (page 94)	Create a succulent garden in a shallow container. Make a butterfly feeding station with fruit. Craft a seed mosaic.
COMMUNITY PARK OR NATURAL AREA LOCATION	Foraged Petal and Leaf Creatures (page 97) Garden-Grown Pigment Paint (page 94) Root Study (page 67) Floral Photography Studio (page 100) Mud Shower Water-Flow Test (page 31)	Write in a plant journal and practice scientific sketching. Do a plant scavenger hunt.
CONTAINER GARDEN	Seed Tape Garden Design (page 43) Ribbon-Wrapped Plant Fort (page 70) The "Water Less, Worry Less" Self-Watering System (page 74)	Make a hanging container garden. Grow a salsa-themed container garden. Plant a butterfly-friendly container garden.

Growing Together in a Garden Classroom

This section gives specific tips for engaging larger groups of students in a classroom setting. The back of the book also has resources, including a Gardening Assignment Chart (page 120) and Gardening Lab Record (page 119), copies of which can be downloaded at: CallistoMedia.com/gardeningforkids.

Collect a library of gardening guides. A class gardening library with resources on everything from watering techniques to making natural dyes will spark ideas and answer research questions. Sample topics might include companion planting guides, local native vegetation guides, vegetable and fruit cookbooks, flower and herb drying guides, and gardening magazines.

Create a class garden agreement. Successfully encouraging exploration, experimenting, and discovery in a large group setting often requires setting respectful boundaries. It is helpful to have a group discussion so that each student can think about how they would like to be treated by their classmates and how they want to use the garden together. The garden agreement might include guidelines such as "Get permission from your group or teacher before picking something," or "Respectfully remove insects; do not kill them." Post the agreement near your growing area for easy reference.

Brainstorm modifications together. Check out the Mix It Up or For a Group tips for ideas on how to adapt projects to fit your classroom learning objectives and individual student interests. Brainstorming sessions allow children to more consciously use the scientific method. Encourage kids to think about different approaches with questions like: "What if we changed . . . ?" and "I wonder what would happen if . . . ?" Use these projects as a starting point for students to design their own experiments and turn their ideas into reality.

Work in teams. Collaborative, project-based learning creates an environment that values every student's strengths. Many of the experiments in this book are designed to be easily used by teams in a classroom setting. For the experiments, dividing your class into teams means each team can change one variable. Some of the projects can be scaled up, with each team assigned to a particular task. For example, you could create a large-scale spiral garden (see page 55) and assign each level's care to different teams.

Find a cause. Connecting a project to a cause gets students motivated, and a motivated student shows improved behavior and attention levels and retains more information. Gardening projects can be linked to everything from bee extinction and native plant habitat loss to global warming and food waste reduction. Can your garden project be part of the solution to a problem?

Invite an expert to talk to your class. Conservation groups, farmers, gardening clubs, nurseries, and even local government agencies are good places to find knowledgeable people to come in and share their expertise and passion. An added benefit of this: Your class will be exposed to new career fields!

Chapter 2

Let's Grow!

Wouldn't it be amazing to step into a place filled with sweet-smelling flowers, refreshing herbs, juicy berries, colorful vegetables, intriguing creatures, and lush leaves? What if you had the power to create a place like this in your backyard? Welcome to the wonderful world of gardening, where the magical power to create is contained in tiny seeds. In this chapter you will learn the parts of a plant, what plants need, which plants are easy to grow, and some handy gardening skills. You will even discover how gardening has the power to teach you science, art, and math. Keep reading to find fascinating facts about plants and discover the key to unlocking gardening magic!

Gardening = Science + Art (with Dirt!)

A little curiosity can take you on a great learning adventure, right in your own backyard. Have you ever wondered how tiny seeds grow into giant trees? Or marveled at the way mud moves through your fingers? Or noticed tiny creatures wriggling, crawling, and creeping? These simple thoughts can lead to big discoveries!

Gardening lets you have fun and get dirty while learning about science, technology, engineering, art, and math—or STEAM. The acronym combines all of those subjects, just like nature does! When you choose which plants to grow, you are thinking about science concepts like climate and soil types. You may need to draw a garden layout or design structures for your plants to climb on, which use engineering and art skills. While you are sorting seeds, measuring rows, and figuring out the best method for watering, you are using math and technology.

What to Know about Plants before You Dig In

Trying things out while growing plants is the best way to learn about gardening and practice STEAM skills, but here are some basics to give you a head start.

Parts of a Plant

A plant is made up of different parts, and knowing what is what will help you in your gardening adventures!

Seed: A miniature developing plant with a protective outer coat

Radicle: The first tiny root to grow from a seed

Epicotyl: The first part of a seedling to break through the soil

Roots: The underground part of the plant that absorbs moisture and nutrients from the soil and anchors the plant in the ground

Crown: Where the stem connects to the roots

Stem: The long section of a plant that supports the leaves, flowers, and fruit

Leaf: The flat offshoot of a stem that absorbs energy from the sun

Bud: A small growth on a plant that will open up and become a leaf or flower

Flower: The part of a plant that produces seeds and pollen

Fruit: The edible part of a flowering plant that contains seeds

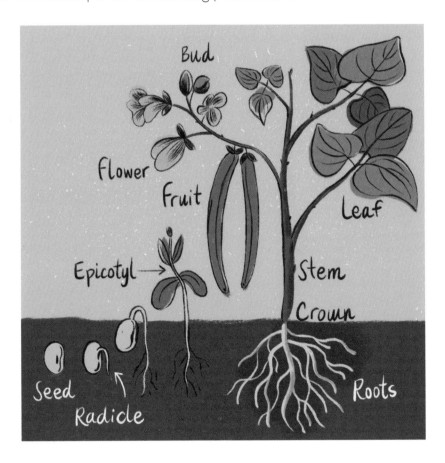

THINK LIKE A SCIENTIST!

Scientists have figured out a powerful way to study and learn things: It's called the *scientific method*. Thinking like a scientist while gardening will help you collect meaningful information, solve problems, and answer questions about the plants you are growing.

Scientists are curious, observant, and ask questions. They are excited to discover why things happen the way they do. Scientists ask questions and then seek answers by experimenting, observing, or measuring—just like gardeners! Gardeners often have questions about why some plants grew well and others did not and how to solve problems with their crops.

Scientists seek information. Research helps scientists understand their subject; gardeners do the same thing. They can find facts written on plant labels and seed packets or look up information in gardening books, websites, and magazines. Scientists have conducted extensive research on plants and everything that affects plant growth, including soil conditions, climate, insects, temperature, and light. You can use what scientists have discovered about plants to try to guess what will happen in your garden.

Scientists predict the answer to their question. Once they have gathered facts, scientists come up with a *hypothesis*, or an educated guess, as to what the solution to their problem might be. Gardeners make educated guesses when they make decisions about where to put their garden, what plants to grow, and when to plant seeds. Wilted sprouts, yellow leaves, holes in leaves, and other gardening problems get solved by making an educated guess about what caused them. Just like a scientist, you can use your prediction to explore, experiment, and find answers!

Scientists test their predictions again and again. Designing an experiment is an exciting step toward finding answers to scientific questions. Professional scientists know that the best experiments change only one thing, called a *variable*, at a time, while keeping everything else the same. By testing one variable at a time, they know for sure that any results they see are due to that one thing and not anything else. Then, they repeat the test again and again to confirm that the first results weren't an accident. If they didn't get the results they were hoping for, they go back and come up with a new hypothesis based on what they learned during their experiment and try, try again. The best way to learn how to garden is to conduct experiments. There are many variables you can test, including light, soil, and water.

Scientists take lots of notes. Scientists record the results of their experiments in great detail. Gardeners do the same! Many use a garden journal (see page 118) to take note of things like when they plant a crop, how healthy the plants are, if there are any insect problems, and whether the crop grew well. Gardeners compare their notes from growing season to growing season so they have an idea of what they should do differently or the same next year.

Scientists aren't afraid to fail. Scientists often find that their predictions were not accurate. But they know that even when they don't get the result they hoped for, they learned something useful from the experiment. Gardeners know that not all of the crops they plant will thrive. But, just like scientists, gardeners solve problems by setting a hypothesis, testing it, recording the results, and repeating the process again. Dig in, make discoveries, ask questions, and don't be afraid to fail! Before you know it, your garden, along with your scientific skills, will grow and bloom.

A Plant's Life Cycle

A plant's life cycle begins with a seed, and all it needs is water, warmth, and air to begin growing. The first thing to grow out of a seed is a root. At this point, the seed is feeding itself with stored nutrients. Then, the first stem and leaf grow out of the seed and push up through the soil. The new seedling can now make food using **photosynthesis**. During photosynthesis, a green chemical in the plant's leaves called **chlorophyll** absorbs energy from sunlight and uses it to turn carbon dioxide (from the air) and water (from the soil) into food. The plant uses this food to grow more leaves and make flowers. Flowers produce seeds that then fall to the ground or get spread by animals. The seeds sprout and start the life cycle all over again.

Handy Gardening Skills

Here are a few helpful gardening skills to know before you grow.

How to Plant a Seed

Your seed packet will tell you when to plant your seeds and how deep and how far apart to plant them. If you are starting seeds indoors, fill your seed-starting containers with potting soil to just below the rim. Make a hole in the soil at the recommended depth, drop your seed in, and then sprinkle more potting soil on top to cover the seed. Tap the containers on a hard surface to settle the soil. Spray the soil with water until thoroughly wet. Mist them when the top layer of soil begins to dry out.

If you are planting seeds outside, either in a container or garden bed, loosen the top 3 inches of soil by raking it or using a garden trowel to turn it over. Use a Popsicle stick to dig rows twice the depth of the seed. Drop your seeds into the rows at the recommended spacing. For tiny seeds, scrape the surface of the soil to make shallow rows. Then, put some seeds in your hand and use a Popsicle stick to gently flick a few seeds at a time into the rows. Cover your seeds lightly with soil. Water until thoroughly saturated. Water whenever the top of the soil is dry to your touch.

10 SUPER EASY AND FUN PLANTS TO GROW

Not sure where to start? Here are 10 of the easiest and most useful plants to grow!

Cherry tomatoes: These fun bite-sized tomatoes come in different colors and are easier to grow than regular tomatoes. They can be planted in containers, in raised beds, or in the ground.

Chives: These can survive all kinds of conditions and are easy to grow from seeds. They taste delicious on baked potatoes, salad, meat, and soup.

Daisies: These flowers come in a rainbow of colors, and their long, easy-to-cut stems make them perfect for bouquets.

Mint: This herb has a well-known taste and smell; it can be grown in a small container or in your garden bed. Use it as an herbal tea, in desserts, or in salads.

Nasturtiums: These fast-growing flowering plants come in many different colors. The entire plant is edible—use its leaves or flowers in salads or sandwiches.

Peas: They grow quickly, are fun to pick and eat right off the vine, and the seeds are easy to handle. If you give them a support structure like sticks, you can even grow them in containers.

Pumpkins: Start these indoors or plant them directly in the garden. There are mini-pumpkins, giant pumpkins, orange pumpkins, white pumpkins, smooth pumpkins, bumpy pumpkins, and many more exciting choices!

Strawberries: These sweet berries can be grown in containers or a huge garden bed. They come back year after year, which means planting one strawberry plant brings you berries for years!

Sunflowers: They come in different colors, sizes, and shapes. Start them indoors in early spring, and after you transplant them into the ground, the larger varieties might get big enough to tower over you.

Sweet potatoes: These plants are so beautiful that some people even grow them as houseplants or in patio containers. Harvest time is like a treasure hunt!

How to Plant a Seedling

Seedlings can be damaged by direct sunlight if they are planted outdoors too quickly. Over three days, place your seedling outdoors in the morning only. Then, your seedling will be strong enough to plant. First, dig a small hole in the ground for your seedling. Make the hole deep enough for the roots; a Popsicle stick works well for digging small holes for tiny seedlings, but a trowel is an excellent choice for larger nursery plants. Next, tip the seed pot sideways, push a Popsicle stick into the soil around the outside edge of your seedling, and carefully push the seedling out of the container into your hand. Finally, place the seedling into the hole and gently push the soil in around its roots. Leave the crown of your plant (the part of your plant where the stem attaches to the roots) above the ground.

How to Water a Plant

Plants can break under pressure from being watered heavily from the top. Use a watering can with a gentle sprinkler head to water new seedlings and garden plants. Swipe the watering can back and forth across the tops of the plants while watering, to avoid washing away too much soil around the base of the plants.

Tools and Materials You'll Need

These are the essential gardening tools and materials you'll need for most tasks. Make sure to check the Tools and Materials sections of each project to see what else you'll need before you dig in. For tools like shovels and trowels, get ones that are the right size for you; they'll be more comfortable and less dangerous to use.

Gloves: Look for a flexible material that has extra protection on the palms. You want to get a pair that fits perfectly. If they're too tight, you can't move well; if they're too big, you can't grab on to things.

Buckets: Get buckets with sturdy, well-attached handles in a few different sizes. Metal handles with a grip last longer and are easier to use than plastic handles. You can also wrap the handles in duct tape for a more cushioned grip.

Gardening scissors: Many garden tasks can be done with scissors. Use them for everything from cutting twine and opening seed packets to snipping off dead leaves and harvesting. Gardening scissors are an excellent choice for kids because they are safer than pruners and fit in small hands. Look for an all-metal utility or bonsai pair of scissors.

Popsicle sticks: Popsicle sticks make perfect plant labels and are helpful for sorting seeds, planting seedlings, and scraping seeds into garden rows.

Trowel: Use this to dig small holes, make planting rows, dig up weeds, harvest root vegetables, and mix compost into garden soil. Look for sturdy metal trowels with wood handles that fit comfortably in your hand.

Shovel: This is a must-have gardening tool for digging, moving dirt and gravel, and mixing compost. Look for a shovel that isn't too long, with a pointed metal head and sturdy wood handle.

Bamboo stakes: These can be used to support plant stems, or you can make a variety of trellis designs from them. Ideally, it's helpful to have a mix of these in different lengths. Look for sturdy stakes that are still slightly flexible.

Garden twine: Great for making a trellis, tying plants to supports, drying herbs, and making bouquets. Look for a label that says "soft twine."

Watering can: Water is heavy, so a small watering can may be more manageable. A good choice is one with a gentle sprinkler head so that young seedlings don't get damaged during watering. A watering can is also useful for feeding plants with fertilizer.

Spray bottle: A gentle way to water a sprouting seed or newly emerged seedling. Get one that has a misting head, not a direct stream spray nozzle.

REPURPOSE AND REUSE!

Instead of visiting a store for gardening supplies, try looking in your recycling bin, closet, office supply drawer, refrigerator, or garage first. There are many items in your home that can be repurposed and reused for gardening. Gardening with repurposed materials saves money and is good for the environment, but best of all, it's fun!

◆ Do you need small pots for planting seeds? You can use toilet paper tubes to make seed pots (see the How Low Can Your Seeds Go? project on page 60). Or, use utility scissors to cut paper egg cartons into individual seed containers. You can also turn a plastic container with a lid into a mini-greenhouse for growing seeds just by adding potting soil.

◆ Do you have new seedlings in the garden that need protection? Cut the bottoms off old water bottles and cover your seedlings with the recycled plastic towers to protect them from slugs, birds, and other things that might eat your new plants. Remove the screw-on lid to create a hole at the top for ventilation.

◆ Are your tomato or squash plants getting heavy and drooping? Cut up an old T-shirt or socks into strips to tie plants to a stake or trellis.

◆ Need a large container for growing potatoes, herbs, or peas? Use an old tote as a grow bag! You can also use an old laundry basket, storage container, or bucket for planting potatoes and other vegetables.

The Dos and Don'ts of Gardening

Before you dig in and start experimenting with gardening, there are a few ground rules to cover that will keep you safe and help you enjoy your time in the garden.

Do be careful about what you eat! Not all plants in a garden are edible. Some, like certain mushrooms and berries, are poisonous. Learn about poisonous plants in your area by checking online or in guidebooks. A good rule of thumb is to ask an adult before you sample anything. And if you have pets, make sure the plants you choose to grow aren't poisonous to them.

Do wear the right clothes for gardening. Working in the garden can mean running into prickly plants, poky sticks, and pointy rocks. Pants let you kneel comfortably, gloves protect your hands when you're working with prickly plants, long sleeves shield you if you are pushing through bushes, and close-toed shoes keep your feet safe in rocky areas.

Do ask for help. There might be times when you need to use pruners, shears, a drill, or permanent glue to do a gardening project. You might know where to find these things, but it is always a good idea to ask a parent or teacher first. They will be happy you asked, and they will be able to help you use it safely.

Don't leave your tools lying around. Tools left outside can hurt someone who accidentally stumbles over them. Putting tools away will also keep them in good condition because they won't get damaged by sun and rust.

Don't go outside without sun protection. You might think you are only going out to the garden for a minute, and then end up staying for hours! Put sunscreen on or use UV-blocking hats and clothing whenever you go outside.

Do "bee" aware. Bees can be helpful pollinators, but it might take some practice to learn how to garden with them buzzing around. Stand still or carefully walk away from bees; do not swat at them.

Part II

GARDENING EXPERIMENTS AND PROJECTS TO DIG INTO

Now comes the fun part—the projects! In chapter 3, you'll find experiments related to starting your garden, from soil testing (page 28) and making seed tape (page 43) to building a Space-Saving Spiral Garden (page 55). In chapter 4, you'll get your hands dirty with garden maintenance projects like The "Water Less, Worry Less" Self-Watering System (page 74) and Ribbon-Wrapped Plant Fort (page 70). Chapter 5 covers the best part—enjoying your harvest! You'll experiment with Strawberry Salsa Science (page 103) and take stunning photos of your flowers with a homemade reflector (page 100). Have fun wandering through the wild world of gardening!

Chapter 3

Observing Your Environment and Starting Your Garden

LOW   HIGH

DIRT-O-METER

TOOLS:

TROWEL

MEASURING CUPS

MATERIALS:

3 GLASS JARS

TAP WATER

DISTILLED WATER

½ CUP WHITE VINEGAR

½ CUP BAKING SODA

SIMPLE FIZZY SOIL TEST

TIME OF YEAR: ANYTIME

DIFFICULTY LEVEL: EASY

PROJECT TIME: 45 MINUTES, PLUS 2 DAYS FOR FINAL RESULTS

- -

Just like the vitamins and minerals in our food help us grow, the nutrients in soil help seeds grow into strong, healthy plants! Some soil has just the right balance and amount of nutrients. Other soil may not, and you may need to **amend** it, or add materials to it, to make it a better environment for your plants. Find out what's in your dirt with these simple soil tests. In this experiment, you'll be observing the different layers in the soil and figuring out its **pH**—whether it's acidic, neutral, or alkaline—with a super-fun fizz test. Once you know what's in your soil, you'll know what, if anything, you need to add before planting. Your skin's pH levels can affect the soil's chemistry, so use a trowel or spoon to collect your sample.

1. Dig down at least 4 inches into the dirt with your trowel to make sure your samples include all the soil layers. Collect 1 cup of soil in each of the glass jars.

Water
Clay
Silt
sand

2. Fill the first jar with tap water almost to the top; leave about ½ inch of empty space. Screw the lid on tightly and shake well. Set it aside for 2 days while the contents settle.

3. Add ½ cup distilled water and the white vinegar to the second jar. Stir it up. Did it fizz? If so, your soil is alkaline.

4. Add ½ cup distilled water and the baking soda to the third jar. Stir it up. Did it fizz? If so, your soil is acidic.

5. No fizz? If you didn't see fizz in either test, your soil is neutral. Most plants grow very well in neutral soil.

6. After 2 days, look at the first jar. The contents should have settled, but the water may be murky, with a few things floating on top. Look closely at the layers of soil in the jar. The top layer is clay: It has fine particles that stick together, making a gooey texture. The next layer is silt, which has

- - - - - - - -
CONTINUED

medium-size particles that settle between the clay and sand. The bottom layer is sand, which has larger and heavier particles. If you look closely at sand, you may be able to see the tiny pieces of rock and hard minerals.

7. Most plants like soil that is 40 percent sand, 40 percent silt, and 20 percent clay. This helps plants get just the right amount of air and water. To find out the percentages of sand, silt, and clay in your soil, first measure the entire soil depth. Then, measure each individual layer, and divide the layer's measurement by the total soil depth. Finally, multiply your answer by 100 to determine that layer's percentage. You can buy clay loam or sandy loam to amend your garden's soil and get it closer to the ideal percentages.

STEAM CONNECTION

In chemistry, pH, which stands for potential hydrogen, is a measurement of how acidic or alkaline a solution is. pH is measured on a scale from 0 to 14, where 7 is neutral, less than 7 is acidic, and more than 7 is alkaline. Check the labels on plants and seeds to discover their ideal pH conditions. Some plants prefer acidic soil, while others like neutral or alkaline soil. You can add products to your soil to raise or lower the pH level. Check your garden store for products called "soil acidifiers" if you need to raise the pH, or look for products like alum to lower it.

FOR A GROUP

Kids can gather soil samples from home and test them as a class. Have them bring in 3 cups of soil in a large resealable plastic bag to test. Look at the results together. Check out a map of your town and compare the test results based on location. Do kids who live close together get similar results? Do they think soil in different areas of their yard might have different properties?

LOW · HIGH

DIRT-O-METER

TOOLS:

PENCIL AND NOTEBOOK

SMALL NAIL

TROWEL OR SPOON

STOPWATCH, OR CLOCK
THAT DISPLAYS SECONDS

DRY AND LIQUID
MEASURING CUPS

MATERIALS:

3 DISPOSABLE, WATER-
RESISTANT BOWLS
WITH WIDE RIMS (WIDE
ENOUGH TO REST ON
THE TOP RIM OF THE
CLEAR BOWLS)

3 CLEAR CONTAINERS,
APPROXIMATELY
16 OUNCES

2 POUNDS SAND

1 POUND
CLAY SUBSTRATE

1 POUND TOPSOIL OR
POTTING SOIL

MUD SHOWER WATER-FLOW TEST

TIME OF YEAR: ANYTIME

DIFFICULTY LEVEL: EASY

PROJECT TIME: 40 MINUTES

- -

Soil contains clay, silt, sand, or a combination of the three. Gardeners know that soil is the foundation for a good crop. They make decisions, like what type of crop to plant and whether they will need a water irrigation system, based on the type of soil they have. This mud shower experiment tests how water moves through different soil types. Which type of soil lets water get to the roots of a plant? Do some soils drain water away too quickly?

1. Get a pencil and notebook ready to record your test results. Across the top of your page, list each soil type: sand, clay, and topsoil. Under each soil type, you'll record the number of seconds it takes for water to start flowing on the first and second tests and the amount of water collected.

2. Turn the 3 disposable bowls upside-down. Use a nail to poke 5 evenly spaced holes in the bottom of each bowl. Be sure the holes are all the same size.

- - - - - - - -

CONTINUED

3. Suspend the disposable bowls inside the clear bowls by resting them on the rims of the clear bowls. Check that there's enough room between the bowls to hold the water draining through.

4. Using a trowel or spoon, put 1½ cups of sand in 1 disposable bowl, 1½ cups of clay in another, and 1½ cups of topsoil in the third.

5. Pour ½ cup of water into the first disposable bowl. Use a stopwatch to time how long it takes the water to start dripping into the clear bowl. Repeat this test for the other 2 soil types and write down how long it takes for the water to flow through each. If no water drains out, write that down, too.

6. Now that the soil is moist, repeat the water test. Add another ½ cup of water to each soil type, testing 1 bowl at a time and writing down the results.

7. Leave the bowls of soil alone to drain. After 10 minutes, measure the water left in each clear bowl: Write down how much water drained through each soil type.

8. Review your results. Some types of soil hold water better than others. Can you tell which type held the most water by looking at how much water drained through? Which soil do you think most plants would like best? Why?

STEAM CONNECTION

This experiment is an example of *soil hydrology*, which is the study of how water flows through soil. Water moves through open spaces in the dirt between tiny soil particles. Some soil, like sand, has large rock and mineral particles that don't fit tightly together so there are large spaces for water to travel through. Other soil, like clay, has tiny particles that fit tightly together, trapping water. Most plants can't survive in standing water; they need soil that drains water away. But if water gets drained away too quickly, the plants don't get enough moisture. A soil hydrology scientist can figure out the best mix of soil types for every kind of environment.

FOR A GROUP

This experiment is fun for a group outdoors where kids can get messy! For younger kids, have other materials like gravel, moss, and leaves available and make it a free exploration activity, allowing them to hold up the bowls and watch the mud shower. How do these materials affect the results? Pair older kids up and explore what happens if you mix the clay, sand, and potting soil together in different ratios. How do the results change? When purchasing materials for groups, plan for ½ pound of each soil type (clay, sand, and topsoil) per child.

LOW   HIGH

DIRT-O-METER

SUN-MAP YOUR GARDEN

TIME OF YEAR: SPRING

DIFFICULTY LEVEL: MEDIUM

PROJECT TIME: 30 MINUTES, PLUS 10 HOURS FOR FINAL RESULTS

- -

TOOLS:

TRIPOD OR OTHER CAMERA SUPPORT (MUSIC STAND, LADDER, ETC.)

TABLET, PHONE, OR DIGITAL CAMERA

PENCIL AND NOTEBOOK

Some plants like to stay in the shade all day, while others want to soak up the sun! When you buy a new plant or seed packet, the label will tell you whether to plant it in full sun, partial sun, or shade. Some plants are so selective about sunshine that the labels even tell you if the plant wants sun in the morning or the afternoon. Do you know what type of sunlight your garden gets? Use time-lapse photography to find the perfect place for picky plants. For a list of programs that help track sun exposure, check the Resources section on page 122.

1. Find a spot you would like to sun-map. On a sunny day (this won't work on an overcast day), set up a tripod facing your chosen spot.

2. Download a time-lapse app on your device that allows you to set the timing for exposures or use a camera with a programmable time-lapse feature or interval-timer mode. If you don't have these tools, you can go out once an hour and take a picture.

3. Set your device on its tripod and focus it on your chosen spot. Don't zoom in too close. Include a little bit of the surrounding landscape so you can compare the lighting on your spot to the lighting around it.

4. Start your time-lapse around 8:00 a.m., or whenever morning light becomes strong. Set your device to take a picture once every hour; stop after 10 hours or whenever the sunlight is low on the horizon. You may be able to program a start and stop time, depending on your device.

5. In your notebook, draw 10 suns that can be colored in with a pencil, 5 for the morning and 5 for the afternoon.

6. Look at each photo in your time-lapse. If you used a phone or tablet, the best way to look at your images is to go into the "Edit" mode. Look closely at the shadows and bright areas in your pictures. If your garden area has full sun, the image will have bright light and any plants in the area will have visible, dark shadows. If your garden area has partial sun, you will see dappled lighting, a mix of dark shadowy and brightly lit areas. If your garden area is in shade, your image will have darker lighting and there will be no visible shadows under the plants in the image.

7. Shade in the 10 suns on your paper to record the type of light at each hour. For full sun, leave the sun unshaded. For partial sun, shade in half of the sun, and for shade, color in the whole sun. Now you know if your garden is good for light-lovers or dark-dwellers!

KEEP IN MIND
Look up what "full sun" means for the plants you want to grow. Often, it may mean 5 hours of sun, not 10 hours of desert sun. If you live in an area that has long daylight hours or intense sunshine, you may need to make an adjustment to the recommendation on the plant label.

CONTINUED

STEAM CONNECTION

Time-lapse photography can be used to make a movie that creates the illusion of time passing quickly. You can use this technique in your garden to observe things that happen too slowly to see. For example, you can take a series of images on a timer over a few days from the same camera angle to capture seedlings emerging through the dirt, or sunflowers tracking the sun. If your device or camera does not automatically compile your time-lapse images into a video, look for a *stop-motion video* app or program. Stop-motion videos combine still photographs into a fast-moving sequence.

DIRT-O-METER

LOW — HIGH

TOOLS:

SCISSORS

MATERIALS:

HEALTHY, LEAFY PLANTS

BLACK PLASTIC
GARBAGE BAG

PAPER CLIPS

LEAF COLOR CHANGE

TIME OF YEAR: SPRING, SUMMER

DIFFICULTY LEVEL: EASY

PROJECT TIME: 20 MINUTES

GROW TIME: 14 DAYS

Have you ever wondered why plants are green?
Chlorophyll is a green substance in plants that absorbs energy from sunlight to make food. Sunlight is made of different-colored wavelengths of light, including all the colors you see in a rainbow. Chlorophyll absorbs mostly blue light but reflects green light, which is why leaves look green. Will a leaf stay green if it isn't exposed to sunlight? Do some plants' leaves stay green longer than others when they're out of the sun? Find out with this experiment!

1. Choose a few different healthy plants with sturdy stems for this experiment but avoid trees. The best results will come from plants that grow in shaded areas with soft, dark-colored leaves, such as hostas, spinach, broccoli, and bok choy. Try to find plants with different kinds of leaves—thick, thin, fuzzy, and glossy.

CONTINUED

2. Use scissors to cut an oval shape from the garbage bag, large enough to cover a leaf of your choice. Make sure to leave an additional inch on all sides. You will end up with 2 identical pieces of plastic, 1 to cover the bottom of the leaf and 1 to cover the top.

3. Cover the leaf with the black plastic pieces by placing 1 on top of the leaf and 1 on the bottom. Attach the plastic pieces to the stem with a paper clip. Place 1 more paper clip at the tip of the leaf and another on one side. Make sure you block all sunlight but keep one side open for airflow.

4. Repeat steps 2 and 3 for each of the plants you've chosen.

5. After 14 days, remove the plastic. What do they look like? How do they differ from the uncovered leaves? What do you think the leaves would look like after more than 14 days without sunlight? What differences do you see among the various plants you chose?

STEAM CONNECTION
Chlorophyll print artists use sun-blocking methods to print images on plants. They have successfully created images on leaves of people's faces, buildings, animals, and landscapes. Research chlorophyll print artists and try out some of their techniques or design your own!

MIX IT UP
Try printing your name on a leaf. Pick a large, soft, dark-colored plant leaf and sandwich it between 2 pieces of clear plexiglass. Using a black permanent marker, write your name on a piece of clear plastic from a sheet protector. Place the plastic sheet with your name between the leaf and the top piece of plexiglass, so your name blocks sunlight from getting to the leaf. Wrap the leaf's stem in a wet paper towel with aluminum foil over it to keep it from drying out and place it in direct sunlight. Check on your leaf in a few days!

LOW   HIGH

DIRT-O-METER

TOOLS:

SPRAY BOTTLE

MATERIALS:

PAPER TOWEL

10 SEEDS

LARGE PLASTIC
BAG OR RECYCLED
PLASTIC CONTAINER

SPROUT-TEST OLD SEEDS

TIME OF YEAR: WINTER, SPRING
DIFFICULTY LEVEL: EASY
PROJECT TIME: 20 MINUTES
GROW TIME: 3 TO 7 DAYS

- -

Wondering if your old seeds are still usable? Use this test to sprout seeds and decide if you should plant them. This sprout test is also a fun way to observe something that's normally underneath the soil: tiny **radicles**, the first part of a seedling to appear as a seed grows. This project is not only a great way to test old seeds, it's also a real-world opportunity to calculate percentages. Pro tip: If you are testing large seeds, soak them for about 8 hours first.

1. Fold the paper towel in half, then open it up and use a spray bottle to lightly mist it with water. Gently place 10 seeds onto one half of the paper towel, then refold it so the seeds are covered. Spray the paper towel again to wet it thoroughly but not to the point that it is dripping.

2. Place the wet paper towel in the plastic bag. Partially close the plastic bag so some air can still get through. If you are using a plastic container, make sure there are a few holes for airflow.

3. Check the seeds each day for signs of sprouting. The very first thing to appear will be a tiny radicle, which looks like a little white tail. That tail will continue to grow and become the plant's root system. Eventually, a green growth will emerge from the opposite side of the seed: This is the first stem and leaf structure. If needed, mist the paper towel to keep the seeds moist. Seeds should sprout within a week or in the amount of time indicated on the seed packet.

4. After a week, count the number of seeds that successfully sprouted: These are seeds that have a radicle. Some of them may have a green growth on the opposite side of the seed, but not necessarily. To count the seed as successfully sprouted, it just needs to have a radicle.

CONTINUED

5. Calculate the percentage of seeds that **germinated**, or sprouted. The reason we used 10 seeds for this experiment is that it is easier to calculate a percentage out of 10. For example, if 4 seeds out of 10 sprouted (4/10), the germination rate is 40 percent. If 8 seeds out of 10 sprouted (8/10), the germination rate is 80 percent. If your germination rate is 80 percent or less, you should either plant more seeds than you normally would or consider getting new seeds. If the germination rate is below 60 percent, it's time to get new seeds.

> ## I DIG IT!
>
> *Germination* is the process a seed goes through to start growing into a plant. Germination happens when everything is just right; the seed has the warmth, air, and water it needs to make its seed coat swell up and break. Seed coats are a barrier to damage, cold, heat, and bacteria. They are adapted to their environment and protect the baby plant until conditions are suitable. When you provide a seed with the perfect mix of water, air, and warmth, you help the seed germinate!

MIX IT UP

Roots grow toward the pull of gravity, while stems grow up and away from gravity—this is known as *geotropism*. See geotropism in action by experimenting with a bean seed. Put the seed in a clear plastic bag with a wet paper towel and staple around the bean to keep it in place. Tape the bag to a window. When the first roots and stem are about 1 inch long, turn the bag a quarter-turn clockwise, and wait for the roots and stem to grow another inch. Repeat until you have made a total of 4 turns and the bag is back in the original position. Can you see how the roots turned each time toward the ground and the stem turned to grow up?

LOW   HIGH

DIRT-O-METER

TOOLS:

MEASURING TAPE

PENCIL AND
GRAPH PAPER

PAINTER'S
TAPE, OPTIONAL

MARKER

RULER

SMALL BOWL

SPOON

PAINTBRUSH

TROWEL

MATERIALS:

TOILET PAPER,
OR OTHER THIN,
BIODEGRADABLE PAPER

SEED PACKETS

FLOUR

SEED TAPE GARDEN DESIGN

TIME OF YEAR: FALL, WINTER, EARLY SPRING

DIFFICULTY LEVEL: MEDIUM

PROJECT TIME: 1 HOUR, PLUS 8 HOURS TO DRY OVERNIGHT

GROW TIME: 2 MONTHS, OR ESTIMATED GROWTH TIME FOR THE
SEEDS YOU USE

- -

Do you dream about delicious produce and dazzling
blooms in the cold winter months? Before planting
season, you can create strips of seed tape with any biodegradable paper. This way your seeds will be perfectly
spaced and ready to roll out in your garden when the
soil warms up. The paper will disintegrate into the soil,
leaving the seeds behind to grow. This method works
especially well for tiny, hard-to-handle seeds, and it
works for any type of garden: in the ground, in raised
beds, and even in containers. Best of all, you can design
your garden layout using seed tape. Arrange seeds by
color, plant type, harvest season, or other themes.

1. Measure the length and width of the area
   where you plan to bury your seed tape. Write
   down the measurements.

- - - - - - - -

CONTINUED

2. What do you want your garden to look like? Which plants do you want to grow together? Which crops can start at the same time of year? Using your measurements of the planting area, plan your garden layout by using graph paper and a pencil. Draw a grid with 1-inch squares on the graph paper that represent 1 square foot of growing space. Sketch pictures of your crops into your grid. You can use simple shapes: circles for tomatoes, long ovals for zucchini, lines for carrots. With your design sketched out, you can start creating seed tape to fit your plan.

3. On a flat surface inside, measure and tear pieces of toilet paper into strips that will fill your planting area. If you have enough space indoors, you can use painter's tape to mark out the dimensions of your planting area.

4. Check the spacing suggestions on the back of your seed packet(s). Use a marker and a ruler to make marks on the toilet paper where the seeds should go. For example, if your seed packet says that seeds should be spaced ½ inch apart, make a small mark every ½ inch.

5. In a small bowl, mix a little flour and water together with a spoon to make a thick paste. Adjust with a little more flour or water as needed until the mixture is gooey and thick. Sprinkle some seeds on top of the paste.

6. Dip a paintbrush into the paste, grabbing a seed with the tip. Then, dab the seed onto the first mark on the paper. Repeat until you get to the end of the strip of paper. You may be able to make more than one row on your strip. Use a marker to write down the names of your seeds on the toilet paper.

7. Leave the seed tape out overnight to dry. The next day, roll it up and place it in a plastic bag for storage. Keep your seed tape in a cool, dry spot like a basement. For easy reference, save the sketch of your garden plan in a garden journal, or place it in the bag with your seed tape.

8. When you are ready to plant, use a trowel to dig a row at the recommended depth for each type of seed. Bury your seed tape. Water the soil until thoroughly moist. Keep the soil moist until your seeds sprout.

STEAM CONNECTION

Creating a garden plan is a fun introduction to *landscape architecture*. Landscape architects design parks, gardens, playgrounds, and school grounds. They need to understand gardening, drawing, math, engineering, and technology and are trained to work with things like steep slopes, retaining walls, plant groupings, wildlife habitats, construction, and stormwater drainage. If you enjoy landscape design, check the Resources section on page 122 for computer-based garden design tools.

FOR A GROUP

Use seed tape to plan out a community or classroom garden. Divide kids into small groups and give them the freedom to design themed garden areas. Or ask each child to bring in their favorite seeds, then study companion planting and match kids up into groups based on which plants grow well together.

LOW   HIGH

DIRT-O-METER

TOOLS:

PENCIL

RULER

FAUCET OR HOSE

2 MEASURING TAPES

MATERIALS:

DUCT TAPE

CLEAR, FLEXIBLE
PLASTIC TUBING,
AT LEAST 15 FEET
AND UP TO 50 FEET
LONG, ABOUT
¾ INCH IN DIAMETER

2 BAMBOO OR WOOD
STAKES OF EQUAL
LENGTH, AROUND
24 INCHES

FOOD COLORING

THE INCREDIBLE LEVELING TUBE

TIME OF YEAR: ANYTIME
DIFFICULTY LEVEL: MEDIUM
PROJECT TIME: 40 MINUTES

- -

Have you ever watched what water does in a cup if you tip the cup sideways? The surface of the water always stays level. This means you can use water to show when two points are at the same level, or height—even around corners and over long distances. Sometimes, gardeners need to place fence posts at the same level in different spots around their garden, or they want to find a level place for their garden bed. This Incredible Leveling Tube can help with that! Note that this tool uses water in an open tube, so water might spill out.

1. Use duct tape to attach one end of the plastic tubing to the top of one stake, leaving about ½ inch of tubing sticking up above the top of the stake. Attach the tubing along the length of the stake in a few places with more duct tape.

2. Attach the other end of the tubing to the other stake in the same way.

3. Place one end of the tube in a sink and hold the other end up to a faucet and fill it with water. Let the water flow through the tubing, pushing all the air bubbles out. When the tube is full of water and there are no visible bubbles, tip about 10 inches of water out of the tube to create some empty space at each end; that way, the water level line can move up and down without spilling water. Color the water with a few drops of food coloring to make it easier to see.

CONTINUED

4. Now you're ready to experiment with your leveling tube! Grab a partner and have them hold one stake while you hold the other. Check your tool by holding both stakes next to each other. Move your stakes up and down and watch the water levels match each other, no matter the height of your stakes.

5. Can you use your leveling tube to determine if the ground is level? You and your partner each need a measuring tape. Put the tip of one stake on the ground so that the tube is sticking up vertically. Hold it in that position while your partner takes the other end of the leveling tube to another spot a few feet away. Your partner should hold their stake in the same vertical position as yours. Then, measure the distance between the ground and the water line in your leveling tube. How does your measurement compare with your partner's? If your measurements are the same, the ground is the same level where you are standing and where your partner is standing. If your measurements are different, then the ground is not level. For example, if your measurement is 5 inches longer than your partner's, then the ground is 5 inches lower where you are than where your partner is standing.

STEAM CONNECTION

Leveling lines are an ancient technology that have been used by builders for centuries to build decks, foundations, and other structures. They allow builders to measure around corners and trees and over long distances. Just as important as finding two level points is knowing when a landscape is not level and locating slopes that could cause erosion and water runoff.

KEEP IN MIND

What happens if you trap air in the tube by putting your thumb over both ends? Does the water level still change if you move the leveling tube up and down? You will probably notice that air bubbles in the tubing will affect the leveling tube. Look carefully for bubbles and, if needed, move the tube until they escape.

DIRT-O-METER

LOW · HIGH

TOOLS:

PERMANENT MARKER

HOT-GLUE GUN OR
STRONG TACKY GLUE
(THIS WILL NEED A BIT
MORE DRYING TIME)

SCISSORS

MATERIALS:

SQUARE TISSUE BOX,
OR OTHER 4½ X
4½ X 5 INCH SQUARE
CARDBOARD BOX

PIECE OF PAPER

30 POPSICLE STICKS

2 PLASTIC
SHEET PROTECTORS

1 GALLON-SIZE PLASTIC
BAG (A THICK, DURABLE
ONE WORKS BEST)

CLEAR PACKING TAPE

ACRYLIC PAINT

POTTING SOIL

SEEDS

MAKE A MINI-GREENHOUSE

TIME OF YEAR: ANYTIME
DIFFICULTY LEVEL: ADVANCED
PROJECT TIME: 2 HOURS, PLUS 1 DAY FOR PAINT TO DRY

- -

Gardeners love greenhouses because they stay warm inside, even in the winter. During the day, sunlight streams through the windows of a greenhouse, keeping the air warm. Greenhouses also trap moisture inside, which helps seedlings grow. This miniature greenhouse uses simple supplies you might already have. Will you use it to sprout seedlings or grow small indoor plants?

 ADULT SUPERVISION ADVISED WHEN USING A HOT-GLUE GUN.

To Make the Greenhouse Windows

1. Use the tissue box as a guide to trace a square onto a piece of paper with your marker. You will use this as a template for laying out your Popsicle sticks.

2. Create a square frame with 4 Popsicle sticks by placing a Popsicle stick along each inside edge of your square template, overlapping the ends of the sticks. Glue the 4 sticks together with the hot-glue gun. Glue a fifth Popsicle stick across the middle of the square frame for stability.

3. Create a support stick that will be pushed into the greenhouse soil to hold your frame in place. Glue this sixth Popsicle stick sticking up from the middle edge of your frame. Your frame should look kind of like a square frying pan with a long handle. Repeat steps 2 and 3 four more times to make a total of 5 frames with long handles.

4. Create clear window panels for your frames. Use the tissue box as a guide to trace a square onto a sheet protector with a marker. Cut along the inside of the squares you drew so you won't see any black lines on your windows! Repeat this step until you have 5 plastic panels. Glue the plastic panels onto each of the wood frames.

- - - - - - - -
CONTINUED

To Make the Base

5. Cut away the top of the tissue box so that you are left with an open-top box.

6. Push the gallon-size bag into the tissue box. Make sure you push the bag into the corners of the box. Cut off the top of the bag, leaving about 1 inch to fold over the top of the box. Use clear packing tape to tape the plastic bag over the edge.

7. Pick a color for your mini-greenhouse. Paint your box with acrylic paint, then let it dry.

To Assemble the Greenhouse

8. Fill the base of the box with potting soil, then push the long handles of your frames into the soil, lining each frame up with one side of the box. Use clear packing tape to fasten the frames together at the corners. You may want to ask someone to hold the frames together while you put tape down the edge. Your window box may be slightly larger than the base of your greenhouse; that's okay. It gives your plant room to grow.

9. The last window frame you made is your roof panel. Set it on top and use it to access the planter.

10. Add details: Popsicle sticks work well for making a door, or use decorative tape along the top edge of the tissue box to cover the edge of the plastic bag. Make 2 more panels to create a peaked roof style if you prefer it over a flat roof.

11. Your greenhouse is ready for seeds and water! Some good seed choices for your greenhouse are lettuce, peas, herbs, spiderwort, polka dot plant, and radishes.

- - - - - - - -
CONTINUED

I DIG IT!

There are many different styles of greenhouses. *Orangeries* grow fruit trees and some even have stoves for heat during the winter. *Conservatories* are decorative glass houses that let you enjoy nature without being outdoors. The world's largest greenhouse domes, sometimes called *biospheres*, have their own ecosystems filled with waterfalls, ponds, fish, birds, forests, and plants.

MIX IT UP

This project is just a starting point! What other materials could you use for your greenhouse? How tall could you make it? What type of roof could you create with more panels? You can also make "stained-glass" greenhouses by coloring some of the clear plastic with markers. If you're feeling ambitious, you can also design greenhouses using things like picture frames, nails, and hinges. For a quicker greenhouse project (great for younger kids), recycle clear plastic containers from the grocery store (e.g., salad or egg containers) and use them as miniature greenhouses for growing seedlings.

LOW | HIGH

DIRT-O-METER

TOOLS:

WHEELBARROW

SMALL SLEDGEHAMMER

TROWEL OR SHOVEL

MATERIALS:

THICK STICKS AND
BRANCHES OF
VARIOUS LENGTHS

GRAVEL OR SAND

TOPSOIL

SPACE-SAVING SPIRAL GARDEN

TIME OF YEAR: FALL, SPRING
DIFFICULTY LEVEL: ADVANCED
PROJECT TIME: 3 HOURS

- -

Play with sticks and branches while you design a whimsical spiral garden! Building vertically gives you more space, and the spiral shape allows you to plant both shade-loving and sun-loving plants in the same area by facing them either away from or toward the sun. Bring your artistic side into the design process by planning how the plants will look together when they've grown.

 ADULT ASSISTANCE REQUIRED WHEN USING SLEDGEHAMMER TO POUND STICKS INTO THE GROUND OR WHEN MOVING HEAVY LOADS.

1. Start by finding a flat spot in your garden or use a raised-bed container. You can use the Incredible Leveling Tube (page 46) to find or make a level spot in your garden.

2. Use a wheelbarrow to collect sticks and branches. You need short sticks (1 to 1½ feet) to start building with and longer ones

- - - - - - - - -
CONTINUED

(2 to 4 feet) to finish. You can also use thick bamboo stakes from a hardware store.

3. Draw a simple spiral shape in the dirt as a guide for your garden. Make the spiral wide enough that you can plant in the space between the lines.

4. Start your spiral design by pushing the smaller sticks into the dirt at the outer end of your spiral shape so they extend just a few inches. Use a small sledgehammer to pound them in if necessary. Every new stick should extend a few inches higher than the previous one.

5. Continue building up the height of your spiral garden using longer sticks as you move toward the center.

6. Use a trowel or shovel to start filling your spiral with a base layer of gravel or sand and another layer of topsoil, at least 12 inches thick. The soil and base material will help hold your design in place. Increase the amount of gravel or sand as you go, ramping up to the center of the spiral.

7. Once you have reached the top and are happy with your design, add more topsoil to fill any gaps. Your spiral garden is ready for plants!

STEAM CONNECTION

Spiral gardens create *microclimates*—areas where the soil moisture, sun exposure, and temperature are very different than in surrounding areas. A good example of a microclimate is a valley in a hot, dry desert. The shade in the valley creates cooler temperatures than the surrounding desert. Cold air sinks into the valley and gets trapped, creating moist air. Just like a small valley, the shady sides of a spiral garden are good for shade-loving plants while the areas facing the sun are good for sun-loving plants.

MIX IT UP

You don't have to stick with sticks when you build a spiral garden: You can use rocks, bricks, large stones, or pavers. Just stack your chosen material up higher as you build from the outside to the inside of your spiral design. You can even make spirals large enough to walk through! Or create several small spiral gardens with themes like herbs, flowers, rainbow colors, butterflies, salsa, or succulents.

Chapter 4

Growing and Maintaining Your Garden

LOW   HIGH

DIRT-O-METER

TOOLS:

SCISSORS

PENCIL

RULER

SPOON

SPRAY BOTTLE

MATERIALS:

PAPER TOWEL AND
TOILET PAPER TUBES

TAPE

POTTING SOIL

SEEDS (PEAS AND BEANS
GROW GOOD SPROUTS)

HOW LOW CAN YOUR SEEDS GO?

TIME OF YEAR: ANYTIME

DIFFICULTY LEVEL: EASY

PROJECT TIME: 45 MINUTES

GROW TIME: 7 TO 14 DAYS

- -

Under a blanket of soil, seeds start sprouting when they feel water and warmth. The growing seeds rely on their own food storage for energy until they reach sunlight. Can seeds grow from deep underground? Experiment with planting depth to find out! Make seed-starting tubes of different lengths and compare your seedling growth between the containers. Do they all sprout?

1. Cut paper towel and toilet paper tubes to different heights so that you have a very long one, a very short one, and a few others in between.

2. Use a pencil and ruler to draw four ¾-inch lines, spaced evenly around the bottom of each tube.

3. Cut along the lines to make 4 slits.

4. Fold the flaps in to close the end of the tube. Overlap each flap, like folding a box. You may

want to push the flaps down flat by poking a pencil inside the tube.
Secure the flaps with a piece of tape.

5. On the outside of each tube, use a ruler to measure up 1 inch from the
   bottom, and mark the spot with a pencil. Use a spoon to place 1 inch of
   soil in each container, then put in your seed. Cover the seed with soil, filling the tube to the top.

6. Place your plantings together in a sunny location. Use a spray bottle to
   heavily moisten the soil, with the same number of squirts for each tube.
   A good experiment tests one thing at a time. Here, you're testing planting
   depth, so keeping everything else the same is important.

- - - - - - - -

CONTINUED

7. Spritz the soil with a little water daily to keep it moist. Check the label of the seed packet for germination time: This is how long it will take before you see a little green seedling growing through the dirt. It may take a little longer than the seed packet's listed time frame because you buried some seeds deeply. Wait about a week longer than the time listed on the seed packet to review your results. Did all of your seeds sprout? Do they look the same? Do all of the seedlings look good, with strong stems and a healthy green color?

I DIG IT!

This seed-growing experiment demonstrates how seedlings need to reach the sunlight quickly to start making food for themselves. The seeds are *dormant* (inactive) until they get what they need: water, air, and warm soil. Most seeds have the same, simple requirements, but some have strange needs! Some seeds need heat from a wildfire to crack their outer coating, while others need smoke from a fire, mixed with rainwater, to germinate.

FOR A GROUP

Split into small groups or partner kids up and test different types of seeds. Will tiny, lightweight seeds be able to grow from the same depths as large seeds? Each group can choose a different type of seed for the experiment and then the whole class can discuss the results. Can they find a correlation between seed size and how deep it can be planted and still germinate?

LOW | HIGH

DIRT-O-METER

TOOLS:

SCISSORS

SHARP KITCHEN KNIFE

MATERIALS:

HERBS (BASIL, MINT, OREGANO, LEMON BALM)

GLASS JARS OR CUPS

POTTING CONTAINERS

POTTING SOIL

LEAFY GREENS (LETTUCE, CABBAGE, CELERY, BOK CHOY)

SHALLOW DISHES

ROOT VEGETABLES (CARROTS, TURNIPS, PARSNIPS, BEETS)

SWEET POTATOES

TOOTHPICKS

FOOD-SCRAP SPROUTING

TIME OF YEAR: SPRING, SUMMER

DIFFICULTY LEVEL: EASY

PROJECT TIME: 20 MINUTES

GROW TIME: 7 TO 14 DAYS

Recycling isn't just for your food packaging; it's for your food, too. Many herbs and vegetables regrow their tops and roots when they are placed in water. Sprouting food scraps is a great way to investigate how plants grow—and you can eat your results! Choose organic veggies to get the best results, as some nonorganic food is chemically treated to prevent sprouting. Check the tops and bottoms of your food scraps for green growth or roots every few days. Use a journal to draw or write about the changes you see (see page 118 for a sample journal page). Once you start regrowing food scraps, you won't want to stop! What other vegetables or plants can you sprout?

 ADULT SUPERVISION OR HELP MAY BE NEEDED WHEN USING A KNIFE TO CUT VEGETABLES.

CONTINUED

To Sprout Leafy Green Herbs

1. Using scissors, cut a long stem, about 4 inches, off an herb plant or fresh, organic herbs from a store. Place the stem in a small glass jar with water, covering the stem only, not the leaves. Keep your stem in a bright location but out of direct sunlight.

2. Change the water daily to keep it fresh. After a few days, roots should appear. Plant your sprouted herb in a container with potting soil when the roots are about 1 inch long.

To Sprout Leafy Greens

1. Using a sharp knife, cut the green tops and most of the stalks off your leafy greens, leaving the pale-colored base intact. (You shouldn't have individual stalks or leaves.) Place the base in a shallow dish of water, but don't submerge the whole base.

2. Change the water daily to keep it fresh. In about one week, roots will begin growing from the bottom, and leaves will sprout from the top. You can plant the sprouted vegetables in the ground or a raised bed or in a container with potting soil when roots are visible.

To Sprout Root Vegetables

1. Because the roots of root vegetables have already grown and been harvested, they will sprout, but you will be growing the leafy tops, not the bottom part of the plant. With a sharp knife, cut the top inch off your root vegetable. Place the cut end in a shallow dish of water.

2. Change the water daily to keep it fresh. In a few days, new green tops will start growing. Once you see roots forming at the base, you can plant the sprouted vegetables in the ground, in a raised bed, or in a container with potting soil. You can harvest the leafy tops until the growing season is over.

To Sprout Sweet Potatoes

1. Using a sharp knife, cut a sweet potato in half. Push 3 or 4 toothpicks into each potato half, around the top.

- - - - - - - -

CONTINUED

2. Place the potato half, cut-end down, into a jar to see if the toothpicks hold it in place. Move the toothpicks around until your potato piece is hanging into the container nicely. Fill the container with water so that half of the potato is wet. Repeat with the other potato half.

3. After a few days, shoots, or slips, will appear out of the top of the sweet potato. When the slips are about an inch long, carefully twist them off. Place the bottoms of the slips in a shallow dish of water in a sunny location. Change the water daily to keep it fresh until the slips form 1-inch roots.

4. Plant the slips into soil, leaving the top half exposed. Sweet potato plants are sensitive, so handle the sprouts gently. The slips should grow into beautiful vining plants. In the fall, you can harvest sweet potatoes from their roots. Use a pitchfork to gently pull the plants up out of the ground and dig around for new sweet potatoes.

STEAM CONNECTION

Engineers are often asked to design things that meet a set of requirements. Can you design food-scrap growing containers? What do your plants need to sprout? Use your creative thinking skills, just like an engineer, to design and build containers that meet your plants' needs.

FOR A GROUP

Food-scrap sprouting is a fun, economical way to start a classroom garden. In the springtime, ask kids to bring in scraps from their favorite vegetables and herbs. Use the methods in this project to help kids grow their scraps. When roots appear, plant them outdoors. You could also conduct an experiment with the class that compares growing a crop from food scraps versus growing it from seeds.

DIRT-O-METER

LOW   HIGH

TOOLS:

PAPER, CLOTH,
OR MESH BAG FOR
COLLECTING SAMPLES

WEED-PULLING TOOL
WITH FORKED END OR
SMALL TROWEL

MAGNIFYING
GLASS, OPTIONAL

PENCIL AND NOTEBOOK

NATIVE PLANT FIELD
GUIDE FOR YOUR
AREA, OPTIONAL

MATERIALS:

OUTDOOR PLANTS

TABLECLOTH OR
BUTCHER PAPER

ROOT STUDY

TIME OF YEAR: SPRING, SUMMER, FALL
DIFFICULTY LEVEL: EASY
PROJECT TIME: 1 HOUR

- -

Roots anchor plants in the ground and suck up nutrients and water from the soil. Have you ever looked carefully at roots? Do flower roots look different than vegetable roots? Do wild weed roots look different than the roots of your garden plants? Dig up a variety of plant samples from outside and compare the roots to find out. If you are digging up plants from a garden, ask for permission before pulling them out. This project works best when soil is moist, like on a rainy day or after watering a garden.

1. Gather several plant samples. To dig them up, loosen the dirt first. Push your weed-pulling tool into the ground a couple of inches away from the main plant, wiggle it around, and push the soil up. Gently pull on the top of the plant while pushing it up out of the ground with your tool. If it has a very long root, you might need to dig deeper. Sometimes, small pieces of the root may break off in the ground—that's okay. Repeat with the other plants you'd like to study.

- - - - - - - - -

CONTINUED

2. Spread your plant samples out on a tablecloth on the ground or on a table and look through them. Do grass roots look different from flower roots? Do wild weed roots look different from the roots of garden plants?

3. Look at the description of root types in the I Dig It! section of this project. Can you spot the plants with long taproots? What about the plants with fibrous roots that branch out all over? Separate your plants into 2 piles according to the type of roots they have.

4. If you have a magnifying glass, look closely at the details on the roots. Use your pencil and notebook to sketch the types of roots you see. You can identify the plants using a field guide or by searching online. Can you see a difference between the roots of plants that grow tall compared to plants that stay low?

I DIG IT!

Plants have two types of roots, either *fibrous roots* or *taproots*. Plants with fibrous roots have a mass of roots that are all about the same size and branch out in different directions. Have you ever pulled up a weed like a dandelion and noticed a very long, thick root? That's a taproot! Plants with taproots have one main root that grows deep into the ground. A taproot also has small roots branching off it called *root hairs*.

MIX IT UP

On a sunny day, you can make shadow art with your root samples! You'll need an unlined piece of paper, a pencil, and a partner. Lay your paper down on a flat surface and have your partner hold one of your root samples up. Move the root around to position it between the sun and the paper, so that it casts a shadow onto your paper. Trace the shape of the root to create an intricate piece of root art.

TAPROOT

FIBROUS ROOT

LOW   HIGH

DIRT-O-METER

TOOLS:

PRUNING SHEARS

SCISSORS

SINGLE-HOLE PUNCH, OR ROUND LEATHER PUNCH TOOL

MATERIALS:

5 BAMBOO STAKES, ½-INCH TO 1-INCH DIAM-ETER, 5 TO 8 FEET LONG

THIN PLASTIC LID FROM A FOOD CONTAINER

COLORFUL STRING, TWINE, RIBBON, OR GARDEN TAPE

SEEDS OR SEEDLINGS FOR VINING PLANTS (CUCUMBERS, SQUASH, PEAS, MORNING GLO-RIES, OR BEANS)

RIBBON-WRAPPED PLANT FORT

TIME OF YEAR: SPRING, SUMMER

DIFFICULTY LEVEL: EASY

PROJECT TIME: 1 HOUR

GROW TIME: 20 DAYS

- -

Create a colorful work of art that also supports vining plants! Gardeners like to grow crops up instead of across the ground—a method called **vertical gardening**—so they can grow more in a small area. Vertical gardening helps create airflow, which minimizes plant diseases. With this easy-to-make plant fort, your plants will enjoy the bene-fits of vertical gardening, and you will enjoy looking at the bright display of string. Don't have an in-ground or raised-bed garden? Don't worry, this project will work for container gardens, too (see the Mix It Up tip).

! THIS PROJECT MAY REQUIRE CUTTING BAMBOO STAKES TO SIZE WITH PRUNING SHEARS. ADULT SUPERVISION SUGGESTED.

1. Choose how tall you would like your fort to be. For the plants suggested for this project, 5- to 8-foot stakes work well. If you need to cut the stakes to the right size, ask for an adult's help with the shears.

2. Use scissors to cut around the inside lip of the plastic lid so that you end up with a flat, round piece of plastic. It doesn't have to be a perfect circle. A circle around 4 inches in diameter will work well for most plant forts.

3. Use a hole punch to create 5 or 6 holes spread evenly apart, close to the center of the plastic circle.

4. Push the bamboo stakes through the holes in the circle. You may need to use scissors or the hole punch to make some of the holes bigger for the larger bamboo stakes. When you get all of the stakes into the circle, you are ready to place your plant fort in the ground.

5. Use one hand to hold the plastic piece with the bamboo stakes together at the top of the stakes. With your other hand, spread the stakes out into a tent shape: Ask for help holding them in place if needed. You can reposition the stakes until you have a shape you like, then push them several inches deep into the soil until they feel secure.

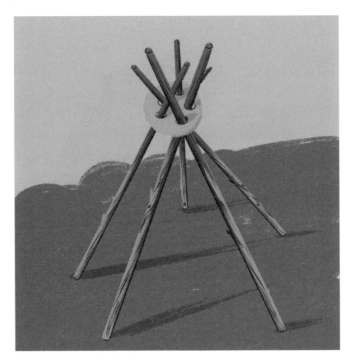

- - - - - - - -
CONTINUED

6. Now make string art! Use colorful string to decorate the bamboo stakes. First, tie a knot to the base of one stake. Then, wrap the string around the stake several times to make a colorful band. Stretch the string over to the next stake, then wrap it again. Repeat as many times as you like. Tie the string in a knot and cut it when you want to switch colors. Fill the fort with a grid of string.

7. Plant seeds or seedlings around the outside base of the fort, close to the stakes. When your plants start growing, take a good look at your design. Is there anything you could change to support your plants better? Do you need to add or cut away any string? Train your plant to grow up your plant fort by gently hooking any tendrils or new vines around the string.

STEAM CONNECTION

Plant forts solve two problems: limited growing space and poor airflow. Anything people design to help solve a problem is considered *technology*. Scientists and engineers often work together to develop new technology for vertical farming. *Hydroponics* is a technology developed to grow plants without soil. Hydroponic gardens have plants that grow vertically, in containers that circulate nutrient-rich water around their roots. Vertical farming technology can help solve problems like food scarcity.

MIX IT UP

You can make a plant fort even if you only have a deck or patio. Use 6 large nursery pots or 5-gallon buckets spread out in a circle. Follow the steps in this activity to make a plant fort, but insert a bamboo pole into each container instead of the ground. Plant your vining vegetables or flowers in the plant pots.

LOW HIGH

DIRT-O-METER

THE "WATER LESS, WORRY LESS" SELF-WATERING SYSTEM

TIME OF YEAR: SPRING, SUMMER

DIFFICULTY LEVEL: MEDIUM

PROJECT TIME: 30 MINUTES, PLUS 1 DAY FOR GLUE TO DRY

Do you wish you could leave your garden for a few days and not worry about returning to thirsty, wilted plants? For centuries, farmers around the world have used clay pots to hold water underground in their gardens. This simple system puts water where plants need it most, at their roots. Water slowly seeps through the pots because clay is **porous**, meaning it has tiny holes that allow water to travel through. As a bonus, this project provides a place to add ornaments to your garden! What will you choose to cover the watering holes of your buried pots? Painted pebbles? Decorative stones? Clay creatures? Use this project to create an artistic and functional garden accessory.

 ADULT HELP AND GUIDANCE SUGGESTED WHEN USING PERMANENT GLUE.

TOOLS:

TROWEL

WATERING CAN WITH A SINGLE SPOUT

MATERIALS:

1 UNGLAZED TERRA-COTTA CLAY POT WITH DRAINAGE HOLE

WATERPROOF, EXPANDING, PERMANENT GLUE, OR SILICONE CAULK

1 UNGLAZED CLAY SAUCER, SAME DIAMETER AS THE TOP EDGE OF YOUR POT

HEAVY STONE OR OTHER HEAVY OBJECT

ACRYLIC PAINT, OPTIONAL

SMALL ROCK, GLASS STONE, OR OVEN-BAKE CLAY

SMALL STICK

1. Check your pot to make sure it is porous. Fill the pot with water, wait an hour, then check to see if the outside is damp. Sometimes clay pots have imperfections that stop moisture from seeping through. If your container is not damp after an hour, do not use it for this project.

2. Following the package directions, spread the glue around the top rim of the clay saucer. Push the top rim of your clay pot onto the saucer's top edge, where you placed the glue.

3. Use a heavy stone to hold the saucer and pot together while the glue dries.

4. Once the glue is fully dry, check to see if there are any gaps and use more glue to fill them in. Let your pot dry overnight.

5. Use the trowel to bury your clay pot in your garden with the narrow end up. If you are adding the clay pot to an existing garden, dig the hole 6 inches away from the base of your plants so the roots don't get damaged. If you are planting in a container, bury the clay pot in the center. For new gardens, plant seeds or seedlings a few inches away from the pot in a circular pattern. The drainage hole should be exposed just above ground level.

6. Use the watering can to pour water into the hole until the pot is filled.

7. Make a creative covering for the watering hole. You can use acrylic paint to decorate a rock, use a glass stone, or create your own garden creature out of oven-bake clay to guard your pot. Or glue a stone to a small stick or dowel that can be used to test the pot's water level.

8. Use a watering can or hose to fill your buried clay pot whenever the water level is low. Check the water level by inserting a stick into the hole on top. If the stick comes out dry, it's time to fill the pot!

KEEP IN MIND

Think about the climate you live in when selecting your terra-cotta pots. If you live in a dry environment, you will want large pots; smaller pots may be better in a wet climate.

- - - - - - - -
CONTINUED

I DIG IT!

Buried clay pots may be an ancient irrigation method, but they are more effective than modern sprinkler watering systems. The water inside each clay pot stays there until the soil dries up and pulls the moisture out. Roots eventually surround and attach themselves to the clay pot, because roots grow toward moisture. These simple buried pots let the plant drink as much or as little water as it wants. Some plants are thirstier than others and will pull more water out of your containers. But you can never under- or overwater when you use buried clay pots.

LOW   HIGH

DIRT-O-METER

TOOLS:

SPOON

UTILITY OR CRAFT KNIFE

PENCIL AND PAPER

RULER

SCISSORS

SPRAY BOTTLE

MATERIALS:

2 SMALL (3-INCH)
SEED POTS

POTTING SOIL

2 TYPES OF
QUICK-SPROUTING SEEDS

2 IDENTICAL CARD-
BOARD SHOEBOXES OR
SHIPPING BOXES WITH
LIDS, AT LEAST 10 TO
14 INCHES LONG

BLACK CARDSTOCK OR
CONSTRUCTION PAPER

CLEAR TAPE

DARK TAPE

AMAZING PLANT RACE

TIME OF YEAR: ANYTIME

DIFFICULTY LEVEL: MEDIUM

PROJECT TIME: 30 MINUTES

GROW TIME: 14 TO 20 DAYS

Planted seeds might be stuck in soil, but when they sprout, they become speedy light-seekers. Grab a partner and race different seedlings through a maze to see which one reaches the light first! Research germination rates, then choose 2 different fast-growing seeds, like beans, peas, pumpkins, or squash, or race 2 different varieties of the same plant. Design 2 identical mazes with a partner and watch the seedlings shoot through their racecourse.

! ADULT SUPERVISION OR ASSISTANCE SUGGESTED FOR USING A UTILITY KNIFE.

1. Use the spoon to fill your seed pots with potting soil and plant 2 seeds in each pot at the depth recommended on the seed packet.

- - - - - - - -

CONTINUED

2. Stand both boxes up on the short ends, making sure that their lids swing open in the same way. Using a utility knife, cut a 3- to 4-inch square hole in the top of each box. The holes should be identical in size and should be placed toward the left or right, not in the center.

3. With your racing partner, decide how many dividers you want to use for your maze. One or two work best, but you can experiment with more. Just make sure you don't block all the light. Sketch your maze out on paper and decide where you'll put the holes in your divider(s). The hole in the first divider should be on the opposite side of the box from the hole at the top. If you use more than 1 divider, alternate where the holes are located. This will ensure your plant has to bend to reach the light.

4. To make your dividers, measure the depth of your boxes with a ruler. Using this measurement and the ruler, draw 2 lines on black cardstock to create a strip whose width matches the depth of the boxes and cut it out. The strip should be longer than the width of your box, but you don't need an exact measurement. Repeat to make the number of divider strips you need.

5. Using scissors, cut square holes in your dividers following the sketch you made. The holes should be least 2 to 3 inches wide.

6. Place your seed pots into the bottom of the boxes. Starting at least 4 inches above the pot, fit the dividers into the boxes by folding the ends and taping the flaps to the inside of the box.

7. Remove the seed pots and hold your finished maze boxes up to the light. If you see any light coming through the edges, cover them with dark tape.

8. Use a spray bottle to thoroughly water the soil in your seed pots. Place them into the boxes, on the opposite side from the first light hole. Close the lid to the mazes and place them in a sunny location, like a windowsill.

9. Keep the soil moist by spritzing it with water every other day, or when it feels dry to the touch. Check the progress of your plants every day. If you get 2 seedlings growing in 1 container, remove the smaller, weaker seedling.

- - - - - - - -
CONTINUED

10. Which seed was the fastest? Do you think the number of turns or the height of your maze affected how quickly your seedling grew? What seeds would you like to "race" next?

STEAM CONNECTION

The biological phenomenon of how a plant moves toward light is known as *phototropism*. If a plant "senses" that one side is receiving more light than the other, the plant cells on the dark side grow faster so that they can get to the light. This causes the stem of the plant to bend.

KEEP IN MIND

Seeds need to soak up plenty of water before they sprout. Speed up sprouting with this gardener's trick: Gently rub the seeds with a piece of fine-grit sandpaper to break through the tough outer layer. Then, soak them overnight and plant them the next day.

LOW HIGH

DIRT-O-METER

TOOLS:

TROWEL

PENCIL AND NOTEBOOK

TAPE MEASURE

MATERIALS:

4 LARGE CONTAINERS, LIKE 5-GALLON BUCKETS, STORAGE TOTES, OR NURSERY POTS

POTTING SOIL

4 TOMATO SEEDLINGS

BAMBOO STICKS OR OTHER SUPPORTS

3 DIFFERENT PLANTS FROM THIS LIST: BASIL, NASTURTIUM, CHIVES, MINT, PARSLEY, MARIGOLDS, LEMON BALM, GARLIC, OR BORAGE

POPSICLE STICKS OR GARDEN LABELS, OPTIONAL

DO YOUR TOMATOES NEED A BEST FRIEND?

TIME OF YEAR: SPRING

DIFFICULTY LEVEL: MEDIUM

PROJECT TIME: 45 MINUTES

GROW TIME: 45 DAYS

- -

Certain plants thrive side by side and help each other, just like best friends! Some gardeners use **companion planting**, a way to experiment with growing different types of plants close to each other, to determine which ones work well together. Sometimes, they find combinations that keep harmful insects away, improve the soil, or even make vegetables taste better. In this experiment, you will try giving some tomato plants a companion while leaving 1 to grow alone. Do you think your tomato plants will grow better with a friend?

1. Fill your containers with potting soil. Then, use a trowel to dig a hole at the center of each container. Your hole should be about as deep as the pots your tomato seedlings are growing in.

- - - - - - - -

CONTINUED

2. Carefully remove your tomato plants from their pots by gently tipping them sideways. Hold on to the base of each tomato plant and slide the pot off the plant's soil and roots. Place the roots into the hole. Use potting soil to fill in around the roots, being careful not to bury the stalk of the plant. Push a bamboo stick into the soil next to each tomato plant to support them as they grow.

3. Give 3 of your tomato plants a friend! Plant 1 companion plant at the base of 3 tomato plants. Leave 1 tomato plant to grow on its own without a companion plant. To make it easier to remember which container has what plants, label each with Popsicle sticks or garden labels.

4. Place the containers in a sunny area. Water them when the top inch of the soil is dry.

5. Check your tomato plants once a week. For each plant, measure and record the height and width of the plants each week, along with any other observations. Are there any insects on your plants? Do any of the plants have leaves that look discolored or have holes in them?

6. When your plants start growing tomatoes, take notes about the number and size of tomatoes on each plant. When they are red and slightly soft, they are ready to harvest! Do the tomatoes from each plant taste the same? Have your friends or family members help with a taste test!

7. Reflect on the notes you took. Did you notice any big differences between the tomato plants? Do you think your tomato plants need a best friend to help them grow? If they grew well with a companion plant, which one did they seem to like best?

STEAM CONNECTION

This experiment is an excellent opportunity to follow the scientific method, all the way through to reflecting on the data. Share your results to help other gardeners in your community.

FOR A GROUP

Try companion planting on a larger scale! The Three Sisters method grows pole beans, corn, and squash together to each plant's benefit. The corn acts as a support for the pole beans, the beans provide nitrogen to the soil, and the large, prickly leaves of the squash plants shade the soil and deter animals and insects. It is a centuries-old technology used historically by Indigenous peoples in the United States and could be studied as part of a social studies lesson.

DIRT-O-METER

LOW HIGH

TOOLS:

TROWEL

SHOVEL

ASSEMBLE A TEAM OF GARDEN SUPERHEROES

TIME OF YEAR: SPRING
DIFFICULTY LEVEL: MEDIUM
PROJECT TIME: 1 HOUR
GROW TIME: 30 DAYS

Attract a group of pest-fighters, productive pollinators, and constructive cleaners to your garden to protect the balance of nature and prevent invasions! Give your team of garden superheroes the food and shelter they need. Research the local insects, bees, and butterflies you would like to attract to your garden and what plants they like best. Then, choose a large planting container or a spot in your garden and get to work engineering an inviting habitat. In the spring, you may be able to purchase helpful local garden insects like ladybugs from your neighborhood garden centers.

To Attract Bees

Many plants, like squash, zucchini, cucumbers, and melons, can't develop fruit without pollinators. Bees are some of the best pollinators, but bees around the world are in trouble. You can help keep them from disappearing by fighting two of their main threats: the loss of food sources and places to nest.

1. Bees love large masses of flowers, so plant these bee favorites in your garden: clover, sunflowers, daisies, Queen Anne's lace, yarrow, pansies, peonies, marigold, chives, nasturtium, borage, and black-eyed Susans.

2. Make a homey environment for the bees in your garden using:

   - Piles of stones or sand;
   - Logs for shelter and nesting;
   - Bare soil in a pot or in the ground;
   - Bundles of paper straws or short bamboo pieces tied together with twine.

To Attract Butterflies

Butterflies, like bees, are plant pollinators that help your garden grow. They need water, food, shelter from wind and heavy rain, and a sunny spot for at least part of the day.

3. Plant some of these butterfly-attracting flowers: milkweed, butterfly weed, daisies, goldenrod, butterfly bush, joe-pye weed, asters, catmint, lavender, pink clover, coneflower, lantana, black-eyed Susan, blazing star, salvia, hollyhocks, sedum, allium, cosmos, and aster.

4. Attract butterflies to your garden with:

   - Flat rocks in a sunny location for butterflies to land on and sun themselves;
   - Shallow water dishes or muddy puddles for butterflies to drink from.

- - - - - - - -

CONTINUED

To Attract Ground Beetles and Ladybugs

If you have aphids or other soft-bodied pests eating your plants, ladybugs and ground beetles can come to the rescue. A single ladybug can eat up to 5,000 aphids in its lifetime! Ground beetles patrol gardens at night to get rid of slugs, snails, ants, and grubs. They are both valuable members of your team of garden superheroes. If you release ladybugs into your garden, do it on a cool evening and mist your plants with water before setting them free.

5. Grow these plants to keep ladybugs happy: dill, cilantro, fennel, caraway, yarrow, tansy, angelica, geraniums, cosmos, garlic, calendula, mint, and coneflowers.

6. Attract ladybugs and ground beetles to your garden with:

   - Large rocks or small logs for beetle hideouts;
   - Vegetable plants;
   - Flowering plants rich in nectar.

I DIG IT!

When you invite helpful insects into your garden, you are practicing *sustainable gardening*. Sustainable gardening means you are willing to work with nature and your environment to reduce waste and harmful chemicals and create a place where nature can thrive. Providing shelter, food, and water for beneficial insects helps support and defend our environment.

KEEP IN MIND

If you want a strong team of helpful insects, you must be willing to avoid using pesticides and insecticides. Insecticides might kill more of your friendly insects than the bad ones. If you have a problem with a plant-eating pest, use a pesticide targeted to that specific pest.

LOW **HIGH**

DIRT-O-METER

TOOLS:

1-INCH HOLE SAW, OR
DRILL WITH ¾-INCH BIT

UTILITY SCISSORS

SHOVEL

GLOVES

MATERIALS:

FOOD-GRADE PLASTIC
BUCKET WITH SCREW-
ON LID

POTTING SOIL
OR COMPOST

KITCHEN AND
GARDEN SCRAPS

SHREDDED PAPER,
TOILET PAPER, PAPER
TOWEL TUBES, OR
PAPER EGG CARTONS

COMPOSTING WORMS
THAT ARE NATIVE TO
YOUR AREA

STORAGE CONTAINERS

WORM TOWER SOIL CONDITIONER

TIME OF YEAR: SPRING, SUMMER

DIFFICULTY LEVEL: ADVANCED

PROJECT TIME: 1.5 HOURS, PLUS 3 TO 6 MONTHS FOR
FIRST COMPOST

Compost looks like soil but is made up of leaves, vegetables, plants, and wood pieces that have broken down into a fine, nutrient-rich mixture. Wondering how to make rich compost for your garden? Invite wiggly worms to work as compost creators with a treat-filled worm tower, also known as **vermicomposting**. If you don't have many wild composting worms, you can purchase some online or from a local worm farm (see Resources on page 122), but avoid invasive species.

! ADULT SUPERVISION OR ASSISTANCE IS REQUIRED FOR USING THE DRILL OR HOLE SAW.

1. Using the hole saw or drill, drill lots of 1-inch holes in the bottom and sides of the plastic bucket: This is how worms will come and go. If you use a drill, you will have to clean up the

edges of your holes. Twist the blade of a pair of utility scissors inside the holes to remove any rough edges.

2. Find a spot in your garden for your worm tower. The best place is next to your vegetable or fruit crops. The worms will travel in and out of the tower, spreading **castings** (worm poop, an excellent fertilizer) in the soil where your plants are growing. Use your shovel to dig a hole that is almost as deep as the height of your bucket.

3. Bury the bucket in the ground. Leave the lip of the bucket, where the handle and lid are attached, a few inches above ground level.

4. Add a few inches of potting soil to the bottom of the bucket. Then add some kitchen and garden scraps on top, including eggshells, raw vegetables and fruit, coffee grounds, flowers, and green leaves. Avoid cooked food, dairy, meat, bones, vinegar, oil, citrus, and juicy produce like watermelon. Then, add a thick blanket of shredded paper. Close the lid and wait a week.

5. After a week, check to see if your scraps are attracting worms. Mix the contents of the bucket around. If you don't see any worms, you can buy composting worms and add them to the bucket.

6. When you have active worms in your worm tower, start adding kitchen and garden scraps at least once a week. Add a 2-inch layer of shredded paper on top every time. Worms use it for bedding, and they actually need more bedding than food.

7. Lift the bedding up weekly to check on your compost and to check the moisture. The top layer can be dry, but the bottom layers should be moist. If you live in a dry climate, you may need to add water to your tower. In very hot or very cold weather, place straw on top of the worm tower to insulate it. After a cold winter, you may want to add additional worms in the spring.

- - - - - - - -

CONTINUED

8. On average, it will take 3 to 6 months before your compost turns into a fine, black material that is ready to use. When your worm tower is three-quarters full of compost, stop feeding your worms for a week.

9. Carefully remove the bedding, worms, and any remaining food, and place it in a container. Scoop the finished compost into another container for use in your garden. Leave a few inches of compost in the worm tower, put the worms, food, and bedding back in, then start the process all over again!

I DIG IT!

Did you know that not all worms are good composters? Composting worms like blue worms and tiger worms live in the top 12 inches of soil and gobble up decaying plants and leaves. By contrast, earthworms burrow deep into the soil and don't come to the top often.

FOR A GROUP

You can install several towers throughout a class and conduct an experiment! Put fruit in one tower and veggies in another so that the worms can move between the two bins. Do the worms seem to like the contents of one bin more than the other?

Chapter 5

Harvesting and Enjoying Your Garden

LOW   HIGH

DIRT-O-METER

TOOLS:

PESTLE

KNIFE OR FOOD PROCESSOR, OPTIONAL

SIEVE OR CHEESECLOTH

PAINTBRUSH

MATERIALS:

SMALL JARS, BOWLS, OR PLASTIC CONTAINERS

FLOWER PETALS, VEGETABLE CUTTINGS, LEAVES

MASKING TAPE AND PERMANENT MARKER

VINEGAR

WATERCOLOR PAPER OR WHITE CARDSTOCK

BOILING WATER

RUBBING ALCOHOL

GARDEN-GROWN PIGMENT PAINT

TIME OF YEAR: SUMMER AND FALL (IN SOME LOCATIONS, SPRING GARDENS MAY OFFER ENOUGH GROWTH FOR THIS EXPERIMENT)

DIFFICULTY LEVEL: MEDIUM

PROJECT TIME: 25 MINUTES, PLUS 1 DAY FOR RESULTS

- -

Have you ever wondered what gives plants their color? Plants produce substances called **pigments**. Pigments make flowers colorful and are essential for attracting pollinators like honeybees, butterflies, and humming-birds. Natural inks, dyes, and paint can be made from colorful vegetables, flowers, fruit, leaves, and weeds. Which plants in your garden make good pigment paint? Can you create a painting of your garden using your homemade garden paints?

 ADULT SUPERVISION IS ADVISED IF YOU ARE USING BOILING WATER AND WHEN YOU ARE DICING HARD VEGETABLES LIKE BEETS OR CARROTS WITH A KNIFE.

1. Take a few small containers into your garden. Gather small pieces of colorful plants such as flower petals, vegetable cuttings, or leaves. Some of the best natural dyes come from plants with deep colors, like red cabbage, dandelions,

marigolds, hibiscus, beets, carrots, and spinach. Keep each sample in a separate container.

2. Use a piece of tape and a permanent marker to label each of the containers with the names of the plants you collected.

3. Mash each sample with a pestle to release the pigment. When you see some moisture coming from your plants, you have mashed them enough. For leafy plants and flower petals, tear the samples before mashing. Hard vegetables like carrots or beets should be diced with a knife or run through a food processor before mashing.

4. Cover the mashed plant samples with vinegar. Use just enough vinegar to get the sample wet. The more vinegar you add, the more watered down and faded the paint color becomes. Leave the plant samples to soak overnight.

5. The next day, strain your paint to get large plant pieces out. Have 1 new container ready for each paint color. For each color, hold a sieve or piece

CONTINUED

of cheesecloth over the new container and pour the paint through. Throw the strained pieces away or into a compost bin. The strained liquid is your new pigment paint.

6. Dip a paintbrush into one of the paints and paint a sample stroke onto your watercolor paper. Label the paint stroke with the plant name. Rinse your paintbrush in a cup of water and repeat, making a sample stroke for each plant. Compare the colors. Which plants had the most colorful pigment?

7. Repeat this experiment using different solvents. Try using boiling water or rubbing alcohol instead of vinegar. Which solvent works best? Is there one solvent that works best for all the plants, or does each plant react better to a different solvent?

STEAM CONNECTION

Studying the way plant material behaves when combined with liquids, like vinegar, is a great way to learn about and test *solvents*. A solvent is a liquid that dissolves other material. In this experiment, vinegar is used as a solvent. When a solvent dissolves and mixes with something, it creates a *solution*. In this experiment, the solution is the paint you made!

FOR A GROUP

As a group, study the historical use of natural dyes. Break into groups and assign each group a basic color like green, yellow, pink, brown, or purple. Blue is a difficult color to make, so it may be better to try after success with the basic colors. Each group can research the best plants to use to make their assigned color, then do this experiment to try to extract that color. Then, combine science and art by sharing the pigment paint to make botanical watercolor art.

DIRT-O-METER

LOW HIGH

TOOLS:

GARDEN SCISSORS

SMALL PAPER, MESH, OR PLASTIC BAG

LARGE PAINTBRUSH, OPTIONAL

MATERIALS:

VARIETY OF NATURAL PLANT PARTS, INCLUDING FLOWER PETALS, LEAVES, BERRIES, VINES, AND BARK

WHITE CARDSTOCK

SCHOOL GLUE, OPTIONAL

CLEAR SEALANT, OPTIONAL

FORAGED PETAL AND LEAF CREATURES

TIME OF YEAR: SPRING, SUMMER, FALL

DIFFICULTY LEVEL: EASY

PROJECT TIME: 20 MINUTES

- -

Plants are an important part of an animal's **habitat**. A habitat is the natural home of a living thing and includes everything it needs to survive. The plants in your garden provide shelter, food, and water to insects and other animals. Who lives in your garden? Do you see beetles, butterflies, and snails? Or maybe lizards, lacewings, and grasshoppers? Recreate a creature from your garden using the textures and colors of plants, or use your imagination to create your own garden creature.

1. Think about the type of creature you would like to create. Will it be a bird? An insect? Or maybe a squirrel, raccoon, snake, or ladybug? What types of plants and colors will you use to create your creature? Do you need something for a beak, eyes, or tail?

- - - - - - - -

CONTINUED

2. Head outside with a pair of garden scissors and a small bag. Collect samples of leaves, flowers, stems, bark, and sticks.

3. Arrange your collected plant parts on a piece of white cardstock. Start with the main body of your creature. Layer plant pieces on the paper to get the shape you'd like. You may need to use scissors to trim the pieces into circles, ovals, and other shapes. Finish your creature by making legs, wings, a tail, and finally the head. For the eyes, you can cut small circles from either a very light or very dark plant piece.

4. When you are happy with your design, you can take a photograph to capture the creature you created and return the plant pieces to nature by scattering them under a bush or tree.

5. If you'd prefer, you can glue everything in place. Carefully lift the bottom layer of your design up slightly and squeeze a bit of glue under it. Repeat for each layer, putting a small dot of glue under each. Let it dry for a few minutes, then use a paintbrush to gently paint a clear sealant over the top of your creature. Make sure you cover all the plant pieces so that they will be preserved and won't change color.

STEAM CONNECTION

This project is a fun introduction to *land art*, a method of creating images, sculptures, and designs from things found in nature. Many artists use photography to document their land art creations so that they can share them with others. Land art can be tiny, or it can be as big as a beach and visible from far away.

KEEP IN MIND

It is helpful to review your local plants online or in a field guide before starting this project. Find out what plants might be poisonous or irritating so you can avoid touching them.

MIX IT UP

Make this into a science activity by challenging your knowledge of local wildlife. Can you create an animal by collecting only plants it uses as food and shelter?

LOW   HIGH

DIRT-O-METER

TOOLS:

LARGE PAINTBRUSH

GARDEN SCISSORS

DIGITAL CAMERA
(A DIGITAL CAMERA ON
A PHONE OR TABLET
WILL ALSO WORK)

MATERIALS:

1 PIECE OF CARDBOARD,
APPROXIMATELY 16 BY
20 INCHES

GLUE STICK

ALUMINUM FOIL

1 LARGE WHITE FOAM-
CORE POSTER BOARD,
APPROXIMATELY 22 BY
28 INCHES

MATTE BLACK
ACRYLIC PAINT

SMALL VASE OR CUP

1 OR 2 SMALL STOOLS
OR BOXES

FLORAL PHOTOGRAPHY STUDIO

TIME OF YEAR: SPRING, SUMMER, FALL

DIFFICULTY LEVEL: EASY

PROJECT TIME: 40 MINUTES

Have you ever noticed how quickly some flowers fade? With a camera, you can capture the beauty in your garden to enjoy forever. Some photographers specialize in **floral photography**. Floral photography captures the colors, patterns, shapes, and tiny details of flowers. You can make a homemade backdrop and light reflector and create amazing flower pictures in your garden with any type of camera.

1. Put the piece of cardboard on the ground or on a table. Spread a generous amount of glue from a glue stick onto one side of the cardboard. Then, tear or cut pieces of aluminum foil and stick them to the cardboard until the whole side is covered. Make sure the shiny side of the foil is facing up. This is your light reflector.

2. Make your backdrop by painting one side of a white foamcore poster board with matte black acrylic paint. It's important that the paint is matte, not glossy. If the first coat doesn't completely cover the white, let it dry, then paint one more coat. The backdrop is double-sided: You can use the black or white side for your photos.

3. Choose a sunny day without wind to take flower photos. Cut some flowers with your scissors and put them into a small vase. Find an area that is mostly shaded but has direct sunlight nearby. Put the vase on a small stool in the shade. Prop the backdrop up behind your flowers; you can choose whether to use the black or white side.

4. You are ready to light your flowers with beautiful reflected sunlight! You might want a partner to help you with this step. Hold your light reflector facing the sun. If you can put the reflector in direct sunlight, that's even better. Slowly pivot your reflector back and forth or up and down until you see a flash of light appear on your flowers. Hold your reflector in that position to keep the light shining on the flowers. Then, get close to the flowers with your camera, crop everything out except the flowers and the background, and take your picture! Experiment with different flowers, different backgrounds, and different positions in your yard.

> **STEAM CONNECTION**
> This project uses several pieces of technology to make art. The reflector is an important tool used by professional photographers. The word *photography* is from Greek and means "to paint with light." By using a reflector to move light onto their subject, photographers really do paint with light!

CONTINUED

FOR A GROUP

Floral photography can be done in a classroom with a sunny window. You'll only need one background board and one reflector if you take turns. Try working in pairs: one reflector holder and one photographer. The final images could become an art display, greeting cards, or a student calendar.

LOW **HIGH**

DIRT-O-METER

TOOLS:

DINNER KNIFE OR NYLON KID'S KNIFE

CUTTING BOARD

MIXING BOWL

LARGE SPOON

PENCIL AND NOTEBOOK

MATERIALS:

2 POUNDS STRAWBERRIES

1 TABLESPOON HONEY

2 TEASPOONS BALSAMIC VINEGAR GLAZE

3 TABLESPOONS LEMON JUICE

1 TABLESPOON OLIVE OIL

¼ TEASPOON SALT

¼ TEASPOON PEPPER

3 LARGE FRESH BASIL LEAVES

TORTILLA CHIPS

STRAWBERRY SALSA SCIENCE

TIME OF YEAR: SUMMER
DIFFICULTY LEVEL: EASY
PROJECT TIME: 20 MINUTES

- -

Your kitchen is like a laboratory where you can experiment with food. Making strawberry salsa is a fun way to play with food chemistry. Salsa recipes mix acidic ingredients with nonacidic ingredients to achieve a tasty balance. Do you like your salsa sweet or spicy? Make this strawberry salsa recipe, then add other flavors until you find your favorite mixture. Serve your salsa with the chips, or with other food like salads, meat, and tacos. Your friends and family will be happy to taste the results of this experiment!

1. Pull or cut the green tops off the strawberries and rinse them under cold water.

2. Slice the strawberries into pieces. First cut them in half, then place them on a cutting board cut-side down. Chop them into large or small pieces; you choose! Put the chopped pieces into a mixing bowl.

- - - - - - - -

CONTINUED

3. Add the honey, balsamic vinegar glaze, lemon juice, olive oil, and salt and pepper.

4. Take the fresh basil leaves and tear them into tiny pieces. Add them to the mixing bowl.

5. Mix all of the ingredients with a large spoon.

6. You are ready to taste your salsa! Sample the salsa with chips. Do you like the mix of flavors? Would you like it to be sweeter, spicier, or saltier?

7. What other flavors would you like to add? Add extra ingredients very slowly: A pinch at a time is a good rule. Keep tasting and stop when you like the flavor. Write down your final mix and proportions of ingredients in your notebook. This way you will be able to share your final recipe! You might be able to find ingredients for your salsa in your garden. A few flavors you can experiment with are cilantro, onions, peppers, jalapeños, and herbs like mint. If you add an ingredient you don't like, you have made a valuable discovery. Professional chefs often make several changes to their recipes before settling on a final list of ingredients.

I DIG IT!

You might know that tomatoes are a fruit, not a vegetable. But did you know that a tomato is a berry, but a strawberry is not a berry? It's true! Strawberries aren't berries because their seeds grow on the outside. Berries grow their seeds on the inside, like a tomato! Each seed on a strawberry is actually a dried fruit that contains its own tiny seeds. An average strawberry has about 200 of these little dried fruits.

FOR A GROUP

Ask your class to participate in an experiment to answer this question: Does adding an acid to salsa improve its flavor? Prepare bowls of chopped ingredients ahead of time. Let each kid invent their own salsa recipe by giving them guidelines. For example, the salsa should include at least 4 ingredients plus 1 added acidic component (either lemon juice or vinegar). Let the students mix their own recipes without adding the acidic element. Have them taste the salsa. Then, add the lemon juice or vinegar and have them taste their salsa again. How did the flavor change? Vote on whether they think acid improves the flavor.

LOW   **HIGH**

DIRT-O-METER

TOOLS:

MASKING TAPE AND PERMANENT MARKER

4 (14-OUNCE) MASON JARS OR FOOD CONTAINERS

WOODEN SPOON

POTATO MASHER

LARGE SOUP LADLE

TIMER

DISH TOWEL

LARGE STOCKPOT OR SAUCEPAN WITH LID

PENCIL AND NOTEBOOK

MATERIALS:

5 CUPS SUGAR

2 POUNDS GRAPES (ABOUT 5½ CUPS)

THE GRAND GRAPE JAM QUEST

TIME OF YEAR: ANYTIME

DIFFICULTY LEVEL: MEDIUM

PROJECT TIME: 1 HOUR 30 MINUTES, PLUS 8 HOURS TO SET JAM

Have you ever wondered how the fruit in jam turns into a thick jelly? Grapes and other fruit have a substance in them called **pectin**. When you combine pectin, acid, sugar, and heat, it causes thickening. Grapes are rich in pectin and acid, so they make great jam! Study the effects of temperature on the natural pectin found in grapes. Will your favorite jam come from cooking your grapes for a few minutes, half an hour, or an hour?

 THIS PROJECT REQUIRES BOILING A HOT MIXTURE ON A STOVE. ADULT SUPERVISION IS SUGGESTED.

1. Every kitchen is different, so you need to find the best jam-cooking time for your kitchen. To keep track of what time gave you the best results, label your jars with cooking times before you start. Place a piece of masking tape on each of the 4 jars. Use a permanent marker to write "10 minutes" on the first jar, "25 minutes" on the second jar, "40 minutes" on the third jar, and "55 minutes" on the fourth jar.

2. Get ready to cook! Set the wooden spoon, potato masher, and sugar out next to your stove. Set the jars and a large soup ladle close to the stove-top, as well as your timer.

3. Rinse the grapes thoroughly with water, and place them on a dish towel. Remove all the grapes from the stems and place them into the pot.

4. Add 2½ cups of water to the pot. Over medium-high heat, heat the mixture until it boils. Turn the heat down to medium and continue to cook until the grapes are soft and squish when you press them with a wooden spoon, up to 10 minutes. Mash the grapes with the potato masher.

5. Keep heating the mixture on medium heat, then slowly add the sugar 1 cup at a time. Stir the sugar continuously until it dissolves. Bring the mixture to a rapid boil. As soon as it begins to boil, set your timer for 10 minutes. Stir the mixture while it is cooking to prevent it from burning. When the timer goes off, use the ladle to fill the jar labeled "10 minutes" with the grape mixture.

6. Set the timer for another 15 minutes, keeping the mixture at a rapid boil and stirring frequently. When the timer goes off, use the ladle to fill the jar labeled "25 minutes" with the mixture.

7. Repeat step 6 two more times, first filling the jar labeled "40 minutes" and then the jar labeled "55 minutes."

8. Place lids on the jam-filled jars and set them in the refrigerator to cool. After 8 hours, your jam will be ready to inspect. Take the jars out and use a spoon to get a sample from each jar. Try each sample. Do they have different textures? Which one works best for spreading? What do you think the jam would be like if you had cooked it longer?

9. Which sample is your favorite? Write down your results so that when you repeat this recipe, you know how long to heat the mixture.

- - - - - - -
CONTINUED

STEAM CONNECTION

Chemistry is the science of combining more than one thing into a new substance, often using heat or a solution like water to break apart and mix different elements. When the grapes are heated with sugar and water, pectin is extracted. Pectin is a carbohydrate that can be used to thicken and make a gel by binding cells of substances together.

MIX IT UP

You can use this recipe to make jams with other fruits that have just the right amount of acid and pectin to thicken well: plums, gooseberries, boysenberries, loganberries, raspberries, passionfruit, and apples (apples have less moisture than grapes, so add 2½ extra cups of water to the recipe for apples).

DIRT-O-METER

LOW HIGH

TOOLS:

HAMMER

SMALL PIECE OF CLAY
OR PUTTY

GARDEN SCISSORS

MATERIALS:

ASSORTMENT OF
12-INCH STICKS

SAWTOOTH PICTURE
HANGER, AROUND
2 INCHES LONG WITH
A NAIL HOLE ON
EACH END

SMALL NAILS

STRONG, TACKY GLUE

ACRYLIC
PAINT, OPTIONAL

TWINE

HERB AND FLOWER DRYING RACK

TIME OF YEAR: SUMMER, FALL

DIFFICULTY LEVEL: MEDIUM

PROJECT TIME: 30 MINUTES

Save your favorite garden plants by hanging them upside down! Gardeners tie herbs and flowers in bundles and hang them so all the good-smelling oils and colors flow down to the tips. You can use dried herbs to cook with, in teas, and for making lotions, soaps, and sachets. This simple drying rack uses natural sticks to create a grid for hanging plants.

 ASK AN ADULT FOR HELP USING THE HAMMER AND NAILS.

1. Collect a bunch of 12-inch sticks. Choose mostly thin sticks, plus 2 larger ones about ½ inch in diameter. Peel off any loose bark and moss. Wash them with dish soap and water and dry them out overnight. If your sticks are damp, the glue will not work well.

CONTINUED

2. Place 1 of the larger sticks on your work surface. Put the picture hanger in the middle of the stick; with an adult's help, use the hammer and 2 small nails to nail it to the stick. This is the most difficult step; adults may need to do this ahead of time for younger kids.

3. Put a piece of clay or putty onto the picture hanger, then push the putty side of the stick down onto your work surface to secure the stick. Place another large stick parallel to your main stick, about 10 inches away.

4. Connect the 2 parallel sticks by laying 2 more sticks vertically between them like a bridge. It should look like a tic-tac-toe game. Glue the sticks together at the points where they intersect. Now that you have a framework for your drying rack, it's time to be creative! Keep gluing sticks in any pattern you would like to make a grid of overlapping sticks. Use plenty of glue to secure the sticks wherever they touch.

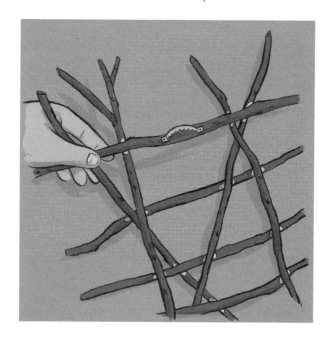

5. When you are done gluing all of the sticks in place, let them dry overnight. You can leave the sticks their natural color, or you can paint them with acrylic paint. When your rack is dry, choose a spot to hang it. Hammer a small nail into the wall and hang your drying rack on the nail head.

6. It's time to dry some herbs or flowers! Some good choices include coneflower, baby's breath, lavender, salvia, yarrow, hydrangea, astilbe, rosebuds, pansies, and any herb like mint, rosemary, oregano, and thyme. Pick herbs and flowers in the morning. Using your garden scissors, cut 5 or 6 inches of the stem when you cut your chosen plant.

7. For flowers, pull the leaves off the stem, leaving the blossom. For herbs, pull the bottom leaves off the stem to make a spot for tying twine.

8. Bundle the stems of your herbs or flowers together and tie them in a double knot with a 9-inch piece of twine. Take the leftover long ends of twine and make a loop by tying them together in a double knot. Use this loop to hang your bundle on the drying rack.

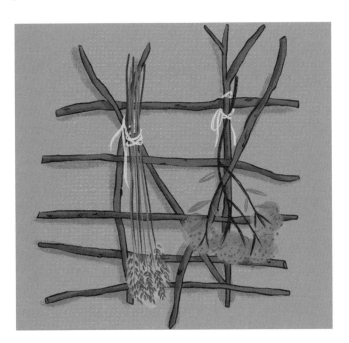

CONTINUED

9. Dry your herbs and flowers in a place that gets good airflow, has average humidity levels, and gets sunlight, but not harsh, direct light. When your bundles are dry, you can put dried flowers in vases, pinch off dried herb leaves and store them in jars or crushed in small containers, or make wreaths, sachets, soaps, or oils with your dried garden plants.

STEAM CONNECTION

Drying is one of the oldest ways to preserve food. Foods that are dried are called *dehydrated*. This drying rack is a simple method for drying flowers and herbs, but scientists have developed sophisticated methods for dehydrating all kinds of food, even ice cream! Dehydrated food won't spoil as easily as other food because mold and bacteria need water to grow. Dehydration removes almost all of the moisture in food.

MIX IT UP

Drying racks can be used to harvest seeds. Wait until the seed heads on herbs or other plants turn brown, then cut a few stems off the main plant. Remove the leaves and petals, but keep the seed head. Tie the stems together and hang them upside down on your drying rack. After a couple of weeks, you can harvest the seeds. Gently pull the seeds with your fingertips or shake the stems over a small container. Store the seeds in an envelope in a dry location until you want to plant them.

LOW HIGH

DIRT-O-METER

TOOLS:

HOT-GLUE GUN AND
GLUE STICK

MATERIALS:

STURDY PLASTIC LID,
LIKE ONE FROM A
PEANUT BUTTER JAR

5 POPSICLE STICKS

STRONG, PERMANENT
GLUE THAT WORKS
ON GLASS

METAL SCREW-ON
RING FROM 14-OUNCE
WIDE-MOUTH MASON JAR

CORK

14-OUNCE WIDE-MOUTH
MASON JAR

NATURAL WOOD STICK,
ABOUT 12 INCHES

PERMANENT MARKERS

SMALL SCREW-IN HOOK

NAIL OR TWINE

BIRDSEED

STAINED-GLASS BIRD FEEDER

TIME OF YEAR: ANYTIME

DIFFICULTY LEVEL: ADVANCED

PROJECT TIME: 1 HOUR, PLUS 8 HOURS OF DRYING TIME FOR
THE GLUE

- -

Would you like help with controlling bugs in your
garden? Birds sometimes have a reputation as nui-
sances in the garden; however, their visits can help
keep a garden healthy and clean. Adding a bird feeder
to a far corner of the garden will distract them from
eating your crops. While eating seeds, they will also
gobble up unwanted insects like mosquitoes, caterpil-
lars, and flies. Birdwatching can be entertaining, too!

 **THIS PROJECT USES PERMANENT GLUE AND A HOT-GLUE GUN.
ADULT SUPERVISION IS SUGGESTED FOR THE GLUING PART OF
THIS PROJECT.**

1. Place the plastic lid on your work surface, with
    the flat top facing down. This is what will hold the
    birdseed, but we need to create a stick grid and
    seed reservoir. Lay the Popsicle sticks out flat in
    a grid pattern across the rim of the plastic lid.
    Run 2 sticks vertically across the lid and 3 sticks
    horizontally.

- - - - - - - -

CONTINUED

2. Use a hot-glue gun to glue the Popsicle sticks in place. Make sure to use plenty of glue! Add extra glue to the joint areas after the first application—you need a strong grid to hold the bird feeder together.

3. Use the permanent glue to glue the metal screw-on ring onto the 3 horizontal Popsicle sticks. The glue must be strong to hold the bird feeder together, so use plenty of it! Set this seed-holding part of the feeder aside and let the glue dry overnight.

4. Use the permanent glue to attach the cork to the bottom of the mason jar. Let the glue dry overnight.

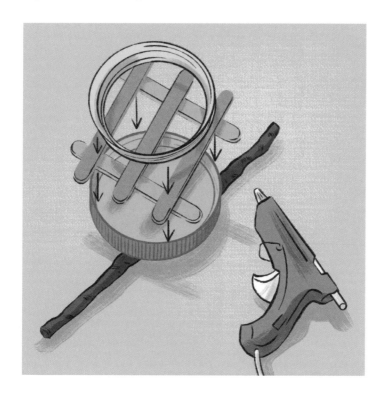

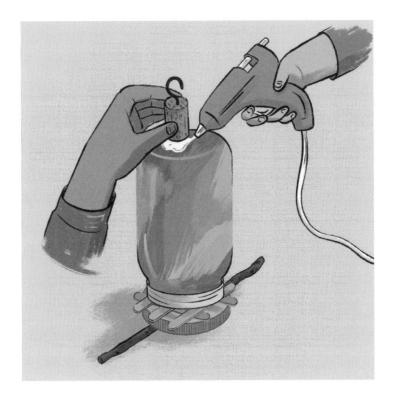

5. The next day, flip the plastic seed-holding lid over and glue the perch onto the bottom of the plastic lid with a hot-glue gun. About 3 inches of the stick should be sticking out from either side of the feeder.

6. Color your mason jar with permanent markers. Get creative and use different colors to make shapes or patterns on the jar.

7. When the marker design is dry, screw the hook into the cork until it is secure. Make sure all of the threads on the screw are fully inserted into the cork. Turn the jar over and fill it halfway with birdseed.

8. Attach the plastic lid with the perch onto the mason jar by placing the metal ring over the mouth of the jar and screwing it on until tight.

- - - - - - - -
CONTINUED

9. Take your bird feeder outside. Carefully flip the feeder over so that the birdseed flows into the plastic lid. Use a nail or loop of twine to hang the bird feeder from its hook in a tree, on a porch, or on a pole in the ground. Enjoy watching birds come to your garden to eat seeds!

STEAM CONNECTION

Scientists who are bird experts are called *ornithologists*. Ornithologists do field studies and record data on everything from bird migration routes to habitat needs. Then, they help make plans for wildlife management, protection, and rehabilitation. Sometimes, gardeners help ornithologists by reporting the kinds of birds they see. Do you know the names of the birds in your garden? If you enjoy birdwatching, you can research local birds, then use a journal to keep track of the birds you spot. You can also check with your local land or wildlife agencies or conservation groups to get involved with bird studies.

MIX IT UP

If you enjoy watching feathered friends, you might want to design a garden patch with plants that attract birds. Birds are especially fond of dogwood trees, holly, sunflowers, sumac, daisy, beautyberry, camellia, columbine, fuchsia, foxglove, lupine, and primrose.

My Garden Journal

This is a blank garden journal template with sections for recording the date, plant name, planting date, and any observations you have.

Name of Plant: ---

Date Planted: ---

Date Transplanted: ---

WHAT DOES MY PLANT LOOK LIKE?	
Date:	
Date:	
Date:	
Date:	

Name of Plant: ---

Date Planted: ---

Date Transplanted: ---

WHAT DOES MY PLANT LOOK LIKE?	
Date:	
Date:	
Date:	
Date:	

Gardening Lab Record

- -

This is a blank template for a scientific assessment, including sections for recording the date, hypothesis, observations, results, and additional questions.

My Experiment: What question am I investigating or testing?

_____

_____

My Hypothesis: What do I predict the answer or result will be?

_____

_____

DATE OR TIME	THING TESTED	OBSERVATIONS/NOTES

Conclusion: What were the results of my experiment, and what was the answer to my question?

_____

_____

Further Investigation: What other questions do I want to test next time I do the experiment?

_____

_____

Gardening Assignment Chart

This is a blank chart that can be used to assign gardening tasks to kids, including weeding, watering, trimming dead leaves, removing insects, and filling the bird feeders/butterfly feeders.

NAME	GARDEN JOB

NAME	GARDEN JOB

Resources

Books

Garden Alchemy, Stephanie Rose, 2020.

Gardening with Less Water, David A. Bainbridge, 2015

Garden of Invention: The Stories of Garden Inventors & Their Innovations, George Drower, The Lyons Press, 2003.

No-Waste Kitchen Gardening: Regrow Your Leftover Greens, Stalks, Seeds, and More, Katie Elzer-Peters, 2018

Vegetable Gardening for Beginners: A Simple Guide to Growing Vegetables at Home, Jill McSheehy, Rockridge Press, 2020.

Worms Eat My Garbage, Mary Appelhof, Joanne Olszewski, Amy Stewart, Storey Publishing, 3 edition, 2017.

The Worm Farmer's Handbook, Rhonda Sherman, Chelsea Green Publishing, 2018.

Websites

Gardening Activities and Educational Resources

Garden lesson plans, blog, garden-based activities: KidsGardening.org

Open-access, peer-reviewed, scientific publications, including research, articles, journals and books. Covers a range of disciplines: ScienceDirect.com

Cornell University College of Agriculture and Life Sciences; a resource for lessons and curriculum based on STEM concepts: Gardening.CALS.Cornell .edu/lessons/curricula/dig-art-cultivating-creativity-in-the-garden

American Society of Landscape Architects; a resource for activity books: ASLA.org/activitybooks

Gardening Zones

US gardening zones: PlantHardiness.ars.usda.gov/PHZMWeb

Worldwide plant hardiness zones: PlantMaps.com

Plant Identification

Largest plant database in the world: DavesGarden.com/guides/pf

Visual identification of poisonous plants: CDC.gov/niosh/topics/plants/identification.html

Visual guide to poisonous plants in the United States and Canada: FWS.gov/uploadedFiles/poisonplantbrochure.pdf

Bees

Nonprofit organizations dedicated to protecting bees: TheHoneyBee Conservancy.org, HoneyLove.org

Printable, state-specific bee identification guides: Pollinator.org/bee-guides

Garden Planning and Design Software

SmallBluePrinter.com

SmartGardener.com

VegetableGardeningOnline.com

3D Modeling

SketchUp.com

Tinkercad.com

Sun Exposure Tracking

Software that will map out the sun exposure for your location:

FindMyShadow.com

SolarDat.UOregon.edu/SunChartProgram.html

Sollumis.com

SunCalc.net

Online Shopping

Seeds and Garden Supplies

Vegetable, herb, and flower seed supplier, organic and non-GMO: store
.UnderwoodGardens.com

Seeds, garden supplies, container gardening: Gurneys.com/category
/flower-seeds-and-bulbs

Seed conservation, seed-saving supplies, and seeds adapted to arid
landscapes: NativeSeeds.org

Garden supply company: Gardeners.com

Seed Savers Exchange: SeedSavers.org

Worm Supplier

UncleJimsWormFarm.com

References

Bainbridge, David A. **Gardening with Less Water**. North Adams, MA: Storey Publishing LLC, 2015.

Baley, Anne. "Benefits of Cinnamon on Plants: Using Cinnamon for Pests, Cuttings, & Fungicide." Gardening Know How. February 15, 2020. GardeningKnowHow .com/garden-how-to/info/using-cinnamon-on-plants.htm.

Cornell University College of Agriculture and Life Sciences. "Dig Art! Cultivating Creativity in the Garden." Learn, Garden & Reflect with Cornell Garden-Based Learning. Gardening.CALS.Cornell.edu/lessons/curricula/dig-art-cultivating -creativity-in-the-garden.

Fernando, Nimal, and Melanie Potock. "Gardening with Kids: How It Affects Your Child's Brain, Body and Soul." PBS. Public Broadcasting Service. March 16, 2016. PBS.org/parents/thrive/gardening-with-kids-how-it-affects-your-childs-brain -body-and-soul.

Growing Great. "Scientific Investigation in the Garden." 2010. GrowingGreat.org /media/garden/9_Scientific_Inquiries.pdf.

The Honeybee Conservancy. "Plant a Bee Garden." August 10, 2019. TheHoneyBeeConservancy.org/plant-a-bee-garden-2.

Kimberton Waldorf School. "Mathematical Arts: Geometry." Kimberton Waldorf School, April 26, 2020. Kimberton.org/geometry.

Langellotto, Gail. "How Science Works: A Guide for Gardeners." Citizen Science (in the Garden!). October 11, 2017. blogs.OregonState.edu/gardencitizenscience /2017/10/11/how-science-works.

Larum, Darcy. "Beneficial Ground Beetles: How to Find Ground Beetle Eggs and Larvae." Gardening Know How. April 8, 2019. GardeningKnowHow.com /garden-how-to/beneficial/ground-beetle-eggs-larvae.htm.

Lester, Stephanie. **Year-Round Project-Based Activities for Stem Grades 1-2**. Edited by Mara Ellen Guckian. Teacher Created Resources, 2013.

McSheehy, Jill. **Vegetable Gardening for Beginners: A Simple Guide to Growing Vegetables at Home**. Emeryville, CA: Rockridge Press, 2020.

Mills-Gray, Susan. "Introducing Food Dehydration." University of Missouri Extension. extension2.Missouri.edu/gh1562.

National Center for Home Food Preservation. "Making Jams and Jellies." March 2017. NCHFP.uga.edu/how/can_07/jam_without_pectin.html.

Pellegrinelli, Carroll. "Basic Recipe for Fresh Fruit Syrup." *The Spruce Eats*. May 29, 2019. TheSpruceEats.com/basic-recipe-for-fresh-fruit-syrup -4108534.

Pereira, Tiffany. "The Chlorophyll Process." *Alternative Photography*. January 20, 2017. AlternativePhotography.com/the-chlorophyll-process.

Pranis, Eve. "Supporting Inquiry—Beyond the Scientific Method." Garden.org. Garden.org/learn/articles/view/942.

Rose, Stephanie. **Garden Alchemy: 80 Recipes and Concoctions for Organic Fertilizers, Plant Elixirs, Potting Mixes, Pest Deterrents, and More**. Beverly, MA: Cool Springs Press, 2020.

Simeone, Vincent A. **Grow More with Less: Sustainable Garden Methods for Great Landscapes: Less Water, Less Work, Less Money**. Minneapolis, MN: Cool Springs Press, 2013.

Tower Garden. "Learning about Parts of a Plant." Tower Garden, n.d. TowerGarden.com/content/dam/towergarden/resources/lesson-plans /grades-2-and-up-plant-roots.pdf.

Index

Acknowledgments

I am grateful for my supportive family. Writing this book meant that they lived in a house with windowsills full of germinating seeds, sprouting lettuce, and potatoes suspended in cups of water. For months, our countertops held bowls of petals, vegetable cuttings, jars filled with topsoil, craft supplies, and endless experiments. My kids—Kayenta, Jade, and Carrick—patiently maneuvered around the mess and let me ask them their opinion about project details without rolling their eyes, even though I'm sure it got old! Daniel, my husband, came through big-time when I needed help leveling a garden plot and moving several heavy loads of gravel. Thank you for giving me the time and space to finish this book.

Thank you to all my friends and family who offered kind words of support, suggestions, and ideas about writing a gardening book for kids. Every thought and experience you shared with me influenced my decisions about what to focus on.

I would not have had the determination, confidence, and courage to tackle a book project without my writing critique partners AJ Irving, Rita Orrell, Angela Dale, and Ami Jackson. I am grateful for Arree Chung and the community he created at Storyteller Academy—thank you for believing in me.

Thank you to Callisto Media for giving me the opportunity to write about something I love. I enjoyed working with every team member and am especially grateful for Ada Fung—you are a gifted editor with a strong sense for valuable and engaging content. And many thanks to Katie Moore—you are an invaluable wordsmith!

About the Author

Brandy Stone is a photographer, writer, and outdoor educator. Her work weaves together the wonder of nature, childhood adventure, and the power of creativity. She has fond childhood memories of adventures outside with her family in Arizona, especially walking across logs, climbing trees, and digging. She enjoys exploring the native plant gardens around her home with the kids who attend her nature-based art programs. She likes hiking but is easily distracted by beautiful scenery, flowers, and other small details along trails. Growing vegetables, herbs, and fruit tucked into natural areas around her home provides endless inspiration and fuels her passion for nature-based art and organic gardening. She develops seasonal art projects and experiments for elementary-aged children, which she shares on her website BrambleGlen.com. She is a mother of three and works from her home in Issaquah, Washington.